My Daughter's
JOURNEY

With Sickle Cell Disease

My Daughter's JOURNEY

With Sickle Cell Disease

Kristin Walker

HEAVENLY MINDED PRODUCTIONS Inc.
New York, New York

My Daughter's Journey with Sickle Cell Disease
Kristin Walker
© June 2014

Publisher: HEAVENLY MINDED PRODUCTIONS Inc.

Email: mydaughtersjourney@yahoo.com
Phone: (718) 986-0075
Facebook address:
https://www.facebook.com/mydaughtersjourney
Editor: Angel M. Barrino, Angel B. Enterprises LLC
Co-Editor: Liza Wright
Co Editor: Marvine Johansen
ISBN: 978-0 9842335-2-6
Cover photo by Sam Gray Photography
Cover design and interior by Juanita Dix • www.designjd.net

Table of Contents

❧

Dedication

⚜

    This book is dedicated to my daughter, Najja, the love of my life. Your spirit has brightened my life. Your smile soothes my soul and enlivens my spirit. You have given meaning to my life. I wake up every day because of you!

    This book is also dedicated to the thousands of children and adults living with Sickle Cell Disease. To the children whose pains are unbearable; who have had strokes and have lost organs. To those who have suffered so much, and had limbs removed; to those who have had countless transfusions, I honor you. To those children on Hydroxyurea and other medication which seems endless, I also dedicate this book to your parents. The time and energy you give to your children is immeasurable. One cannot begin to fathom the endless love and patience you bestow upon them. I urge you to be hopeful about your children's health as they can live healthy, normal lives in spite of the disease. My prayers and my heart go out to you. Your children's lives have purpose and I would like to share my daughter's story with you and your children.

Acknowledgments

Najja's new life would not have been possible without the help of a magnificent team of physicians, nurses and family members. The chain of doctors included:

♦ Dr. Sawicki, her pediatrician. She became a part of Najja's journey when Najja was only a few days old. Dr. Sawicki walked into my hospital room a few days after I had given birth to Najja and immediately there was something about her that struck me. Since that day, seventeen years ago, she has been Najja's primary care doctor. Dr. Sawicki is innovative, knowledgeable, resourceful, patient and caring. She is amazing because she has always shown a deep concern for Najja and her health. She constantly follows up with me to make sure Najja progresses well and that her medical plan is being followed.

♦ Dr. Sadanandan, Najja's Hematologist. Dr. Sadanandan is passionate about her patients and her work, she thinks out of the box. She is resourceful, accessible and easy to talk to.

♦ Dr. Schubert (Dr. S), Najja's Neurologist, very detail in her thinking extremely professional and concern.

♦ Dr. Goodrich. Dr. G. Najja's Neurosurgeon, an amazing doctor; phenomenal in his thinking, dedicated, knowledgeable and insightful.

♦ Dr. Del Toro, Najja's attending Hematologist during the Bone Marrow Transplant. A visionary and compassionate about his work. He is humble in his spirit, steadfast and dedicated to the community of children under his care. Najja was truly blessed to have had Dr. Del Toro as one of her care provider. Dr. Del Toro, you will always have a special place in our hearts.

♦ Dr. R., Najja's Hematologist during the Bone Marrow Transplant procedure. Attentive, kind and support and insightful.

I sincerely thank this team of doctors for going above and beyond their call of duty to change Najja's life. They were insightful, convicted and committed to her cause and to improve her quality of life. There are no words to express my heartfelt gratitude for the treatment and care Najja received as she battled Sickle Cell Disease. Each of you was attentive, supportive and dedicated to Najja's journey to good health. You will always remain invaluable to our family for giving Najja a new lease on life.

TO MY FAMILY:

♦ To my mother who did not waiver, she is always by my side continuously supporting, guiding and encouraging and loving me unconditionally. During Najja's journey with the disease, mom always kept Najja in the forefront of her mind; whenever Najja was sick she was always there to lend a helping hand. Mom I can't thank you enough.

♦ To my daughter Tishanna, who is a spirit of encouragement and believed in her heart that Najja would be cured from Sickle Cell Disease. Tishanna stayed prayerful and faithful to God, trusting that He was working things out on Najja behalf. Thank you Tishanna for your strong faith, love and support.

♦ To my daughter Aisha, whose steadfast spirit kept me grounded and encouraged. In the times when my spirit waivered and my heart ached, she would pray and remind me that; "This too shall pass" During transplant, Aisha stayed with Najja many days and nights, watching, waiting, praying and comforting; keeping Najja uplifted.

♦ To my mother-in-law who also stayed by Najja's side as she journeyed through the transplant. Thank you for your help, Mom.

♦ To my sister Venice and my brother Norman, thank you for your love and support.

♦ To Edmonde, Najja's God mother, thank you for going beyond your call of duty; passionately nurturing and always being available when Najja needed you. We are forever grateful for the seventeen years of your time you gave to us.

♦ To my niece, Shani, your visits, your smiles and love for Najja was a blessing. Thank you, Shan.

♦ To my Husband, the journey was long and tumultuous. You hung in there with me, with Najja. We made it, she made it. Thank you my love for your support and strength.

xii | My Daughter's Journey With Sickle Cell Disease

♦ To Justin, What can I say to you? You are truly a gift from God to Najja and our family. I must share with you my readers, that when I found out that I was having Justin, I was shocked and unsure what to do. This was because Najja was only eight weeks old at that time. I wondered why this was happening. What I did not know was that God had a plan, a perfect plan for Justin to be a blessing to Najja. Justin, you are truly loved and appreciated. I pray for you every day that God will continue to be your source your guide and strength. I love you, Justin.

SPECIAL THANKS TO:

♦ My friend Sharron, Faye and my cousin Juliet for your input and support.

♦ Marvine Johansen for your support and encouragement to write Najja's story.

Introduction

Before I began writing this book, I gave it a lot of thought. I questioned whether I should write it because I did not know who would read it. I wondered if it would benefit a mother, a child, a grandmother; whether it would help an individual living with or caring for someone with Sickle Cell Disease. What I do know is I have a story to share, about being a mother of a child with Sickle Cell Disease.

Within this story you find all the things I learned about the disease; the journey of how I cared for my daughter during this difficult time. You see the process of seeking the right medical care, choosing the right providers and the decisions made concerning medications suitable for her. I write to tell others the important things I learned medically and how she was cured of the disease. Here is my daughter's story:

My daughter Najja is now 17 years old and she had Sickle Cell Disease. Najja is my third child and is the youngest girl. There are two older girls, Tishanna age 34 (she has no trace of the disease or the trait) and Aisha age 31 (she has the sickle trait). My son Justin now 16, is the youngest and has no trace of the disease or trait.

Sickle Cell Disease is a genetic red blood cell disorder. It is inherited from parent to child. The red blood cells of individuals with Sickle Cell Disease are shaped like a sickle or crescent moon. As a result of the abnormal shape of these cells, oxygen and blood cannot move easily through the tiny blood vessel, thus causing painful crisis (crises are painful episodes in different joints because there is not enough oxygen reaching those parts of the body), damaged organs or even strokes.

In order for a child to have the actual disease, both parents (mother and father) must have the trait or must have the disease. It should be noted when both parents have the trait, it does not mean all the children will have the disease but it does mean that some of the children born to parents with this genetic make up will end up with the disease as in my case.

My husband and I have Sickle Cell Trait. What did that mean for us and our children? With each pregnancy, there was a one in four or 25% chance of our baby having Sickle Cell Disease, (all sickle hemoglobin). Or a 50% chance of our baby having Sickle Cell Trait, a mixture of normal and sickle hemoglobin. Or a 25%, one in four chance of our baby having normal hemoglobin, no trace of the disease or trait. In a case where one parent has the trait and the other parent has normal hemoglobin, with each pregnancy there is a 50% chance that the baby would have normal hemoglobin or a 50% chance the baby will have Sickle Cell Trait. None of the children born to such a couple will have Sickle Cell Disease. If both parents have the disease, all the children born to such a couple would have Sickle Cell Disease. If one parent has the disease and the other parent has the trait, there is a 50% chance with each pregnancy the baby would have the trait or a 50% chance the baby will have the disease. There is no chance any child born to such a couple will have normal hemoglobin.

I remember the first time I heard about Sickle Cell Disease. It was in 1981 when I was pregnant with my second daughter Aisha. The obstetrician who provided care for me told me I had the Sickle Cell Trait. Of course I did not have a clue as to what he meant. I gave him a puzzled look as he explained what it meant to have Sickle Cell Trait. Without going into great details, he said it is an inherited red blood cell disorder that came from one of my parents. He said most people with the trait were not affected by it and lived normal lives. The doctor inquired if I knew which of my parents had the trait. I told him I did not know because this was my first time hearing about this disease. He also asked if the baby's father had the trait and I told him that I did not know. He suggested I find out because this information would be important. He further explained if my child's father did not have the trait I would not have to explore the matter any further.

As recommended by my doctor, I spoke to my child's father concerning the issue. He assured me he did not have it because he recently had a blood screening and the result showed no indications of any blood disorder.

I spoke to my mother about having the Sickle Cell Trait. She asked, "What is that and where did you get it from?" I explained, "based on the results from recent blood work, there is an indication I have the trait." Further, "according to my doctor, it is an inherited red blood cell disorder, and I could have only gotten it from one of my parents." My mother immediately said it was not her or anyone on her side of the family, so it must be my father. I spoke to my father and had the same conversation with him as I had with my mother. I asked him if he had Sickle Cell Trait. Like my mother, he had never heard of the disease or the trait so he declared it must be my mother. The conversation about

Sickle Cell Disease and the trait ended there since both of my parents seemed to be in denial.

The next time I heard about Sickle Cell Disease, was during college. I took a health class and the professor discussed a number of inherited diseases; one of them happened to be Sickle Cell. The discussion was in depth and very detailed, so my understanding of the disease became much clearer. Still I had no need to research it any further.

It was not until the disease directly impacted my life that I researched more about it. As I spoke to more people about the disease, I realized many parents and ordinary people had very little knowledge about it. As a result I felt deep in my soul I needed to share my daughter's experience and the things I learned about the disease. In my heart I knew people should have greater insight and understanding as to what living with Sickle Cell Disease and similar illnesses is like. Therefore, let me tell you a little about our experience.

During my pregnancy I learned many things about this disease and the effect it has on the individuals who have it. Driven to learn about its origin, who it affects, how it impacts people's lives and what is being done to help those people, it became my passion to research this illness.

Soon I found out, many people knew little about this illness and there were some who had strong misconceptions concerning Sickle Cell. Yet I want to tell you what Sickle Cell is instead of focusing on what it is not.

Najja's Pre-Natal Journey

❧❧❧

My daughter's journey began long before her birth. Two years before her birth, my fiancé Paul (now my husband) talked about having a child. He, more so than I, had the yearning for a baby. This was because I was the mother of two teenage girls already. Therefore, the thought of having another baby sounded wonderful in my heart but not logical in my head. From my point of view, I felt having a child is a gift from God. It is not a right or something one does because you have the ability to. It is a special gift I felt I must be prepared for on all levels, emotionally, mentally, and financially. With this in my mind, I told him I needed time to think about it before moving forward to make such a commitment.

It took about a year before I actually made up my mind, so in the Fall of 1994 I decided to get pregnant. We tried for about nine months but I was unable to conceive. In 1995, I decided to consult with a fertility specialist on Long Island. On my first visit, a history of my medical background was noted, blood was drawn to check hormone levels and a physical exam was done in order to check my uterus and cervix for any abnormalities. After the examination, the doctor indicated that my reproductive system appeared to be healthy; however he needed to do further testing for blockage in my fallopian tubes.

Approximately one week after my first visit, I was scheduled to return to the doctor's office for the second test. The procedure was done by using a fluid to flush through my fallopian tubes to see if they functioned properly. The results from all the tests came back normal. I asked the doctor what the next step would be since the results from the tests were normal. He recommended a possible procedure called exploratory surgery. This is a surgical procedure that would explore the reproductive system for any signs of abnormalities. I hesitated for a moment then I told him I needed a few days to give it some thought. I went home and spoke to my fiancé about the procedure and also spoke to another fertility specialist. As a result of the information I gathered, I decided to move forward with the procedure. I called the doctor to schedule the appointment for the end of August 1995. Before the actual appointment date, I returned to the doctor's office for blood work. Two days after the blood tests, I received a phone call from the doctor saying, "Some people will do anything to avoid exploratory surgery," he said. I asked him what he meant. "You're pregnant!" he said. I screamed, "You're kidding me! Oh my God! Oh, my God!" This was great news. I was overjoyed, my heart thumped with excitement. I immediately called my fiancé to share the good news. He was also excited. This was the news we anticipated for the past year.

I waited about two weeks before I called an OB/GYN to schedule my first appointment. By this time, it was about mid-September 1995. The day of the appointment came and I was excited of course. When I arrived to the office, there was lots of paper work, blood work questions, and the usual pre-screening before seeing the doctor. Once I was with the doctor, she asked even more questions before she did the physical exam. When the exam was finished, she told me everything appeared to be fine and I should return in a month.

The month ran by quickly and before I knew it I was back in her office for my second appointment. The same routine procedures were followed and again she told me everything seemed to be going well and I should schedule my next appointment for the following month.

During the next visit, something changed, the doctor informed me that my blood work showed I had Sickle Cell Trait. I told her I already knew that, but I never really gave it a second thought because there was no medical disturbance from it, I had not been affected. She suggested I check to see if my fiancé had the trait also. I initially told her that I did not think so, because he had never mentioned it to me; however, I would check with him. I left her office feeling a little uneasy. As I reached home, I called him and shared with him that my doctor noted that I had Sickle Cell Trait and she wanted to know if he had the trait too. He responded by saying he wasn't sure because his doctor had never mentioned it to him. The next day he called his doctor to find out if he was ever tested for having Sickle Cell Trait or disease. His doctor said he would check his records and get back to him. Two days later, he received the phone call from his doctor confirming that he had the trait. Upon hearing the news, my heart dropped, and anxiety crept in. Like most couples we never thought we needed to discuss Sickle Cell Disease.

The next day, reluctantly, I called my doctor and told her that my fiancé did have the trait. She told us since we both had the trait, there was a 25% possibility the baby would have the disease. As the words left her mouth and hit my ears, I immediately felt as though someone sucked the air from my body; I felt numb. She explained, from her experience, children who had Sickle Cell Disease were usually very sick. They were in and out of the hospital frequently for various reasons. She shared a story about a family with a toddler who endured several blood transfusions. She added that there was another family who had two children with the disease and one of the children had a stroke by the age of seven. She discussed other children who had their spleens removed because they became enlarged. She also said for some children, their hands and feet would swell because they were not receiving enough oxygen in those parts of their bodies. This is called the Hand-Foot Syndrome. Hand-Foot syndrome occurs when sickled cells block the small blood vessels in the hands and feet. As a result, the patient experiences pain, swelling and fever.

She explained most of these children did not live normal lives because they experience frequent painful crises. The pain can occur in the legs, arms, back, stomach, hips and fingers; many times the patient experiences pain throughout his or her entire body. She also explained that some children have died at a young age. Her words struck my ears and my heart like a lightning bolt and I was in awe. I wanted to cry but I could not. I wanted to scream, but I could not. I wanted to tear up her words and dump them in the garbage, but I could not. Everything appeared to be at a stand still.

At the end of the conversation, I hung up the phone and went into my bathroom and shut the door. I sat on the edge of my bathtub and began to rock back and forth. Thoughts were rambling through my head like a tornado through a field. I began to question God. I wanted to know why me, why, why my baby? Why was I being punished, what did I do to deserve this? I was numb.

My fiancé knocked on the door and wanted to know if I was ok, but I told him no. I needed a moment to think. I reached for the door knob and unlocked the door. He came into the bathroom and sat next to me. We sat on the edge of the tub for a moment then he reached into his pocket and took out his phone and called his best friend's wife who was a nurse. He began to tell her what the doctor had told us. She responded by saying the doctor was right. "Children with this disease do live painful lives. They spend a lot of time in the hospital because they were usually sick." She added that she also knew a young man with the disease who died by the time he was nineteen. She painted such a grim picture. My fiancé looked at me and said, "I do not think it is a good idea to go through with this pregnancy." He added, "I do not want my child to die before me." Though I listened to his opinion, I did not hear a word he said. I walked off and went to bed in a very somber mood. I felt helpless. I knew I had a long and difficult journey ahead of me.

That journey began the next day. I received a call from my doctor. She advised me to make an appointment to see a Genetic Counselor. She said she knew of a place in Queens named Madina Perinatal Service. This was a place where all types of genetic counseling and testing were done. I took the number from her and made the call immediately and I was able to get an appointment for two weeks later, on December 12, 1995.

On the day of the appointment, we met with a woman named Jamie Lewis who was the Genetic Counselor. She invited us to sit down and discussed the history of Sickle Cell Disease, which groups of people were affected by it, how it is passed from parent to child and how a child would get the disease as opposed to the trait. She discussed the different kinds of Sickle Cell Diseases, which stemmed from mild to severe. She explained that there were various types of Sickle Cell Disease which affect people. She explained that the disease not only affected people of African descent but it affects individuals from the Mediterranean, Middle East, Southeast Asia, Caribbean, Central and South America. She added people from these regions are affected by the various types of the disease. One type she mentioned was Sickle Cell SC. She said this was the mildest type of Sickle Cell and most people with this type have only minor health problems. Other types of Sickle Cell Disease include Sickle Beta Thalassemia Disease. Individuals who are born with this type of Sickle Cell Disease have serious complications. They are prone to infections and other illnesses that require frequent hospitalizations. Then the most serious type is Sickle Cell SS. Individuals born with this type of Sickle Cell Disease have all red blood cells which are sickled shaped and it is the sickling of these cells that cause a host of life threatening problems; these individuals have even more serious complications; are prone to infections, enlarged spleens and frequent hospitalizations as well.

Next she talked about living with the disease. She discussed some of the difficulties parents face. She made it very clear that children living with Sickle Cell Disease usually have many health issues. This is because the disease causes the red blood cells to become sickle shaped, hard, and sticky. As the cells move through the tiny blood vessels they stick together, causing a lack of oxygen and blood flow to particular areas in the body; such as the legs, feet, hands, chest, lungs, back or stomach. When these areas cannot get enough oxygen or blood flow, they release a chemical that causes pain. These pains are known as Sickle Cell Crisis. She explained that the pain ranges from mild and annoying to furiously excruciating. These pains could last from a few days to a few weeks. Many times the children have to be hospitalized because the pain is unbearable.

She talked about Hand and Foot Syndrome which affects young children. She explained when the small blood vessels in the hands and feet become blocked, pain, swelling and fever can develop.

Next, she talked about a condition called Acute Chest Syndrome. She said sickled cells can get trapped in the lungs. This can cause a person to have, fever, difficulty breathing, coughing and severe chest pain and sometimes death."

She talked about the affects the disease may have on the liver. She said sickled cells can get trapped in the liver resulting in scarring and injury to the organ. She explained if the liver gets damaged it causes pain and the white part of the eyes turn yellow. She discussed the spleen which is responsible for cleaning the blood and fighting infection. In Sickle Cell children, their spleens get damaged and have to be removed; as a result, the children are often prone to infections. She said the kidneys, which are responsible for removing waste or extra fluid out of the blood, forming urine and balancing salt in the body, can get damaged. She added that strokes were a common problem for children with Sickle Cell Disease. The strokes were usually caused by a blockage of the blood vessels carrying oxygen to the brain. When a stroke occurs, it is usually a devastating event because the child typically suffers severe brain damage or dies. She clarified that there are a host of other physical problems affecting children with Sickle Cell Disease. These children typically spend days in the hospital; they are usually weak, tired and listless. They are usually smaller than their peers and withdrawn. Physical activities are usually limited because it is very difficult for them to play for extended periods of time. As she spoke, her voice became an echo in my ears. I wanted to go home. I was overwhelmed, sad and sickened by all I had heard. Finally, I stood up and told her I had heard enough and could not listen any longer. Before we left the office, she said I had to take at least two different tests to confirm the baby had the disease. The first test would be an amniocentesis, which could test for several types of genetic diseases and the second would be another type of genetic screening. She stated she would set the appointments and call me with the dates. I thanked her and we left the office.

I felt emotionally and mentally drained when we arrived home; instead of talking I went to sleep. The next morning I got up and went to the kitchen. My fiancé was preparing something to eat, we both looked at each other but we could not say anything because we did not know what to say. We both needed time to think so we just left for work.

While at work, I realized I had a friend who I could speak with. She was the perfect person for me to talk to, I thought, because she had three children, two had the disease and one had the trait. On my break, I called her and briefly explained the importance of my call.

Luckily she was off that day and said I could come over that afternoon. I anxiously waited for the school day to end, which for me was 2:45 p.m. I rushed to my car and drove as quickly as I could to her house, which was one block from where I lived. When I arrived to her house, I greeted her with a hug because I had not seen her for a while. We immediately sat down and I explained to her what was happening. I told her of the conversation I had with my doctor and the latest conversation with the Genetic Counselor and all the things that were said. When I was finished, she said she was told similar things but because she was a nurse her perspective was different.

From her experience with her children, caring for them did require extra effort. When I asked her what she meant; she said, she made sure that they ate healthy foods. Lots of green, leafy vegetables, fresh fruits and lots of fluids, like 100% fruit juices, water, and soy milk (her preference). Water was particularly important because it helped to prevent the cells from sticking together allowing the blood to flow more easily. She said children with Sickle Cell Disease go into crisis often because the blood vessels are blocked; drinking plenty of water helped the cells to flow more freely. I asked her how much water she gives her children daily. She told me that she gave them one cup of water based on every six pounds of their body weight. Her son weighed 60lbs. and her daughter weighed 35lbs. I explained that the Genetic Counselor talked about crisis and I wanted to know whether her children experienced crisis a lot and she told me not often. She mentioned her son had experienced five painful crises that year and the pains were mostly in his legs and stomach. She also mentioned that his pains usually came when he did not drink a lot; adding that the pains were short lived and she was able to treat him at home with Tylenol and a warm compress most of the time.

She said she noticed that when the weather changed, both children usually became sick. They would get fevers, colds and sometimes minor aches. For example from summer into fall she had to watch them closely. As the fall came closer, she dressed them in warmer clothing. As winter came she dressed them in layers because the cold seemed to affect them more. She made it clear it was not an easy job, and sometimes caring for them became overwhelming but she stood firm and did what she had to do, like any parent.

She continued that there are many children living with all kinds of diseases, birth defects and other illnesses and many were surviving. As a parent with two children having the disease, she treated them like any other children. She took the necessary precautions as any parent would do by trying to keep them healthy as possible.

She pointed out in her field she saw many children and adults with the disease. Many of them suffer excruciating pains and often times were very sick. Some had major adverse effects resulting from poor diet and inadequate health care. She made sure her kids ate properly at all times. They drank plenty of fluids each day even when they went to school. She usually packed the amount of fluids that they must drink while they were away from home. She also made sure that they followed a medical care plan. They received regular check ups and current immunizations; vitamins and supplements were given daily. She also made sure their teachers or anyone who may be responsible for their care were aware of what to do if they became sick. Most importantly, even though they were young, she made sure they were aware of how to care for themselves. She said education was the key.

After speaking with my friend, I felt reassured and ready to talk to my fiancé. I needed to convince him having this baby would be a blessing and we could take care of the child.

When I went home I told him I was ready to talk. He did not say much but he was ready to listen. I began to share with him all the things my friend and I discussed including the ways in which she cared for her children and what daily life was like having two children with this disease.

At the completion of my conversation, he shared his thoughts. He disagreed with my position. He felt having a child with such a devastating disease did not make sense. To him, the child would have a painful and poor quality of life which would affect us on all levels. He felt that caring for this child would be difficult and it would be stressful. He said I was using my emotions instead of logic to make my decision. He even asked if I had heard anything my doctor, the Genetic Counselor, or his friend's wife had said. From his point of view, an abortion was the answer because this baby's life could be extremely difficult. As he ended his conversation, I turned and walked away feeling sad and disappointed. I was emotionally torn and did not know what to do; he was just angry.

I called my mom just to talk and share with her some of the things that had transpired between he and I. As we spoke, she sensed the sadness in my voice so she asked me what I wanted to do. I told her I believed in my heart and I felt in my soul that I should keep this baby. My mom said, "Baby, I want you to get down on your knees and pray." "Pray as hard as you can." "Ask God to step into this situation." "Ask Him to make a way because the Word says, 'ask and it shall be given.'" "I took her advice and prayed but things just seemed to worsen. He and I could not come to an agreement about this matter so the arguments became frequent and harsh. As a result, stress and frustration became a part of my daily life and I could not handle it any more. I had reached my breaking point and contemplated having an abortion.

One day I sat down and told him that I thought of having an abortion because I did not have his support. I did not want to take this route but things were not getting easier and I needed his support. I told him I would make a decision after having the amniocentesis done. I told him if the results showed the baby had Sickle Cell Disease I would consider having an abortion. The test was scheduled for December 17, 1995.

I went to the Perinatal Center and took the amniocentesis test. The test was performed by inserting a long needle into my stomach through the amniotic sac. A small amount of fluid was drawn through the needle and was sent to a lab to be tested for several types of genetic diseases. Upon completion of the test, I was told the results should be available within ten days. A feeling of anxiety overwhelmed me and I could not sleep or eat as I waited for the results to come back.

On December 27, 1995, approximately 5:15 pm, I received a phone call from a Genetic Counselor confirming my worst fear. My baby had Sickle Cell Disease and it was the most serious of them, Sickle Cell SS. As he spoke my mouth fell open, my heart stopped and my eyes filled with tears. I could not speak because there was a knot in my throat. I was in shock. I was dumbfounded and numb; a myriad of emotions swept over me. With my back against my bedroom wall, I gradually slid down to the floor and began to wail with tears. Words could not describe how I felt. After a few moments, I called my fiancé and asked him to come home. When he walked in, I told him what the counselor said. The tears were flowing down my face like water from a broken dam. My world had crumbled around me and I felt abandoned and alone, though he was there. He did not interrupt me; as I spoke, he simply listened. After I was finished, he said he was sorry. He asked what I wanted to do. I paused and told him I did not know, I needed time to think. He told me again he could not cope with a child having such a lifelong illness. He said it did not make sense to have a child who would be sick or in the hospital all the time. He reminded me of how unhappy this child would be thus causing us to be miserable. He suggested I terminate the pregnancy as it seemed to be the only logical solution for everyone. I could not say nothing, I just looked at him.

On December 29, 1995, I had an appointment to take another type of DNA test. This test was just a test to confirm the prior results. I had to wait a week for the results. Anxiously I waited yet in the back of my mind I hoped this second result would be different. I hoped it would come back negative and my baby would not have Sickle Cell Disease. When I received the call that the results were back and the test reconfirmed my baby had Sickle Cell Disease, I simply cried for days. It seemed I could not stop crying. My fiancé, however, did not change his mind, because in his mind the solution was clear.

Feeling despair I prayed. I asked God to intervene because I could not fix this situation. I told Him I did not know what to do because I was in a state of confusion and I needed help and direction. I had to make a decision as to whether I should go through with the pregnancy or terminate it. I was 4 ½ months pregnant and my baby was real.

As the days passed, my fiancé and I argued over when I would terminate the pregnancy. He insisted I get it done immediately because the longer I waited the more difficult it would be. I remained resistant and indecisive. My heart, soul and spirit said yes even though I knew the implications. I heard everything he and others said but I wanted to hold my baby, care for her and take the life journey no matter the cost.

After spending a few more days contemplating and fighting with my fiancé (Paul) about the abortion, I became overwhelmed and discouraged, and decided to end the pregnancy.

On January 4, 1996, I called a GYN doctor whose office was located at a hospital in downtown Brooklyn. I explained the entire situation to him. He asked me if I was sure of my decision. He explained to me terminating a pregnancy in the second trimester was a different process. He said the process would take two days. The first day would include counseling, an ultrasound and lab work. In addition, he would have to examine me and more than likely insert cervical dilators into the opening of my cervix. He added there was no medication for this part of the process. I would be sent home with a prescription for pain medication. On day two, I would return for the actual removal of the pregnancy which is done under general anesthesia. He said I would have to arrive early in the morning because the procedure took anywhere from two to four hours.

As he spoke, my lower lip trembled and my eyes filled with tears. He told me to think carefully about my decision and get back to him the following day. The next day, I called the doctor and told him that I had made the decision to go ahead with the termination of the pregnancy. He advised me to come in and talk to him on January 6th but there was a heavy snow storm and he postponed the appointment. He rescheduled it for January 8th, two days later. When we spoke he sensed the apprehension and sadness in my voice. He told me I should think further about my decision before I go through with the procedure.

After my conversation with the doctor, I called my mother. I told her I had made a decision to terminate the pregnancy and I had an appointment to meet with the doctor to discuss the matter further. Upon hearing what I had decided to do, my mother was shocked. She said I could not be serious and I should not go through with it. She told me she was looking forward to her granddaughter being born and I should rethink my decision. I explained to her I did not have Paul's support and I did not think I wanted to go through a pregnancy and raise another child by myself; especially a child that would probably face many medical challenges. I went on to explain to her that Paul felt the baby's quality of life would be difficult and he didn't think it made sense to have a child that would be sick on a constant basis. I told her that he had heard so many negative things from my doctor and his friends about children with Sickle Cell Disease that he felt she would only have a stressful and painful life.

My mother reminded me, "There is a God who rules from above with a hand of power and a heart of love." She continued to quote inspiration based on scripture such as, "Things that are impossible with man are possible with God." She said, "God can do more than we can ever think or imagine, all we have to do is pray, trust God and be faithful." She said, "prayer changes things so I should pray like I have never prayed before!" She continued to encourage me to ask God to take my situation and turn it around. "Tell Him you need Him to show up and do the things He knows how to do," she added.

I took her advice and I began to pray. I said, "God I know that I probably don't deserve your mercy, but I need you, I need you! I need you to give me peace! I need you to help me to make the right decision. I need you to show me the way. I reminded God "One year ago, I asked you for a child and you gave me a daughter. What do I do now?" I went to bed that night crying uncontrollably.

The morning of the procedure, I woke up at 5:00 a.m., I picked up my Bible and went to the bathroom and I began to pray. I chose Psalm 22. "My God, my God, why hast though forsaken me? Why art thou so far from helping me?" I implored. I cried and humbled myself and asked Him to help. I went back to bed and was silent.

To my surprise, Paul woke up and asked me if I was ok. I said, "no." He said that he was having a hard time with the whole situation. He said that he found it difficult to have a child that would be sick for a life time but then he took a deep breath and said, "I will support you, because I know you don't want to do this." "It is frightening, I just don't want our baby to have a difficult life. I don't want her to be sick or die at an early age." He hugged me and I began to cry. I looked up and said "Thank you Lord! Thank you Lord for hearing and answering my prayer." I was relieved, overjoyed and most of all thankful. I waited for the doctor's office to open to call and cancel the appointment.

By the time I was six months pregnant, something new happened. One day while at work, I began to feel a dull ache on the lower side of my uterus. I did not pay attention to it but it continued throughout the day. I left work and went to school, yet still had the same needling pain.

After school, I went home and called my doctor. I explained to her what I felt and the length of time I felt the pain. Based on what I explained to her she advised me to come to the hospital so I could be examined and monitored. I waited for a few hours, but the pain did not go away so I finally decided to go to the hospital. When I arrived, the normal procedures were followed. The nurses took my vital signs and then I was hooked up to the monitor in order for the doctor to figure out what was going on with the baby.

After a few hours of monitoring, it was determined I was actually in premature labor. This was very scary news because I was only six months pregnant. My health provider decided admission was necessary to stop the labor. I was given various medications in efforts to stop the labor, but the medications did not work. Finally my doctor gave me another medication which stopped the labor. I stayed in the hospital for about seven days and was released. I was given strict instructions by my doctor not to return to work, because I was in danger of going into pre-term labor again and it would be dangerous, not only for me, but also for the baby.

I stayed home for another two weeks (March 1-15). After I was given the permission by my doctor, I returned to work. Within a month of returning to work something was wrong again. This time I went to my doctor. After my examination and an ultrasound, I was told that I had Placenta previa. This is a condition which the placenta blocks the passage way of my cervix, leaving no way for the baby to leave the womb. The doctor said she had to see whether the cervix was blocked half way or fully blocked. If it was fully blocked, the longest I could take the pregnancy would be the 39th week and would have to have a C-Section. She reassured me that everything would be fine, because I was in good health and my baby was developing well. After hearing her encouraging words, I felt a bit at ease. I thanked her and left the office. As I walked to my car, I began to talk to God, asking Him, for strength and guidance as I journeyed through my pregnancy. Despite the roadblocks I thanked Him for his presence and for helping me to weather the storms.

The remaining ten weeks of pregnancy went by with minimal complications and on May 29, 1996 at 1:45 pm, Najja (as you see by this time we knew we were having a girl and we had named her) came into the world by C-Section birth. "Oh God! She was lovely!" I was so excited to see her, hold, and smell her! But this was not possible because I was under sedation. However, I kept my eyes on her, as I sighed with joy and relief. Over the next day, I felt better, and was able to hold and feed her. I began to think about how to care for her, once I arrived home.

1996

Her first month, I was not sure what to expect. In my head, I tried to figure out if she was different from any other baby. I watched her very carefully, and handled her with extreme care.

The weeks flew by and before I knew it, Najja was two months old. She had a scheduled appointment to see a hematologist. She needed to get a newborn screening to confirm that she had Sickle Cell Disease. A few days after the screening, the result came back confirming what we already knew. Though I was not surprised by the result, I was saddened. My oldest daughter, Tishanna, who was 17 years old at the time, saw my sadness and she shared some words of wisdom. She said, "Mommy, Najja is a miracle baby! God has given her to us so you don't have anything to worry about because He's got this one." With those wise words I closed my eyes, took a deep breath and agreed to, "Let go and let God!"

Her first year of life was overwhelming for me, even though her development was great! She was hospitalized about three times. She was six months old the first time she became sick. It was November 7, 1996. I was at work when I received a call from my sitter (Edmonde). In a very nervous voice she said, "something is wrong with the baby, but I do not know what is wrong." Edmonde told me she was unable to stop Najja from crying. I asked her what she thought triggered this. She thought the baby had a fever, but she did not know how high the fever was. Immediately I went into my principal's office to let her know that my baby was sick and I had to leave. Once I arrived home, I took the baby from Edmonde and tried to comfort her myself. However, she continued to cry so I told Edmonde to get ready because we had to get the baby to the doctor's office. She quickly dressed Najja and we left for the doctor's office.

Once we reached the doctor's office, Najja was seen immediately! The routine examination was done and blood was drawn. The doctor could not find any physical evidence as to what might be causing the baby to cry so she decided to admit her for observation. Upon hearing this, my heart sank and tears filled my eyes; I was stressed and scared. I wanted to know the reason for admitting Najja, so I asked. The doctors felt it was necessary for them to observe Najja for a few days to make sure she had no underlining illnesses or infections.

One month later, December 17, 1996 Najja was back in the hospital again due to a high fever. As the previous hospitalization, she was admitted so her fever could be monitored and be treated for underlining infections. She was given IV fluids to maintain her fluid levels and antibiotics to fight any infection. She was released after four days.

1997

By April of 1997 Najja was eleven months old. She had been admitted to the hospital for having a fever of 104.2. During the admission, I asked the doctor why Najja had frequent fevers. The doctor explained children with Sickle Cell Disease usually get high fevers because they are prone to infections. As a result they must be treated immediately to avoid further complications.

1998

The next time Najja was hospitalized was one year later, April 1998. She was 23 months old. This time she had a fever for about two days without subsiding. She had to be hospitalized for three days for observation and treatment before she was released. Apart from the fevers, she had not had any Sickle Cell Disease related complications.

It was another twelve months (July 1999) before Najja was hospitalized again. This time she had an inexplicable stomach pain which caused her to cry for long periods of time. She kept telling me, "Mommy, my tummy hurts." It was somewhat difficult to get her to explain any further what the pain felt like because she did not have enough words in her vocabulary to give details. Due to the continual pain, I decided to take her to the emergency room. Once we arrived, she was seen immediately and the necessary blood work, urinalysis and physical examination was done. The emergency room physician concluded she had a stomach virus and it would be necessary that she be admitted for a few days for observation and in the meantime, she would be given IV fluids to maintain her hydration levels.

1999

On December 31, 1999, we had an astonishing experience. Najja was then three years and seven months old. For the first time, she felt the pains of Sickle Cell Disease and we faced what it meant to see our child go through the pains of this disease. It was unbelievable! I was dumbfounded! It was actually New Year's Eve and we were at a friend's home getting ready to celebrate the New Year. Najja was in another room playing with her brother and two other children. Suddenly I heard a gut-wrenching scream. Puzzled, I looked at my husband. The screams came in succession so I ran from the kitchen and yelled Najja's name.

When I reached her, she was sitting on the floor and I asked her what was wrong; yet she could not answer; she was crying too hard. I picked her up and pleaded with her to try to tell me what was wrong. I said, "Baby! Please tell me what's wrong." Finally she was able to say to me, "Mommy my back hurts." My husband was standing behind me and I told him I thought she was in crisis. He took her from me and said, "Let's go!" We headed straight to the emergency room.

The entire trip to the hospital was excruciating for Najja and me. She cried so hard! She wiggled and grabbed my shirt. She continuously asked me to help her and pleaded, "make the pain stop mommy." I couldn't imagine what the pain was like and my heart sank deep into my chest. All I could do was hold her tightly and rub her aching back. Over and over again, she kept saying, "Mommy it hurts! Mommy it hurts!" At times the pain was so intense that she buried her face in my neck and screamed. It seemed as if something was biting deep into her bones.

When we finally arrived to the hospital, I went straight to the admitting window. I explained to the nurse that I thought my daughter was in crisis. At first she looked at me as if she did not know what I was talking about. I repeated myself, but this time indicating that my daughter had Sickle Cell Disease and I thought she was having a crisis. At this point, Najja was crying even louder. The nurse told me to bring her inside to the admitting area and I placed her on a small bed so the doctor could examine her. The doctor wanted to know how many crises she had before that one. I told him none and I explained this was her first time feeling the painful effects of the disease. He wanted to know if she had any transfusions. I told him no. I explained that she had been hospitalized about five times in the past for high fevers.

As he examined her, he decided to do routine lab work to check her hemoglobin levels and a urine analysis. He indicated to us depending on the results from both tests, he would make a decision as to whether it would be necessary to admit her. We waited for a few hours for the results to come back. Once the labs were back, the doctor reported to us that the results were normal in that she did not have any sign of infections and her hemoglobin was an 8.1 which was normal for her. He also added that since she had stopped crying and she had no fever, he decided admission was unnecessary.

2000

By April 12, 2000, Najja was three years and eleven months old. This time she had a painful crisis in her stomach. She cried so intensely, I had to take her to the hospital immediately. This time I took her to a different hospital on Long Island. When we arrived, she was immediately checked in and the routine procedures were followed; an IV was given, urine was taken and blood work done to check her hemoglobin level; she was also checked for infection. We waited for a few hours for the results of the blood and urine tests. Once the results came back, the doctors informed me that everything was within normal range and there were no sign of infections. The doctor also asked me if I could pinpoint the time frame of when the pains would begin to when they ended. I told him that the length of time was usually anywhere from 20 minutes to 30 minutes. He said he was curious because a pain episode usually lasted anywhere from an hour to days at a time. He added that I should continue to document the frequency of Najja's fevers, the crises and their duration.

About four days later, April 16th, I returned to the hospital because Najja complained of chest pains. Again, she was admitted for observation and while we were there, a chest x-ray was done to check for any signs of pneumonia. Additionally, several blood tests were done to check for infections. This time she was admitted for three days. She was discharged because the blood work showed no sign of infection.

By May 10th Najja had another admission to the hospital. This time, she contracted a virus known as Rotavirus. This virus surfaced that year and many children caught it including Najja and her brother (by this time I had my fourth child Justin). Najja was very sick from it. She vomited continuously; she was limp, weak, and listless. She was hospitalized in Long Island and her 2½ year old brother was in a hospital in Brooklyn since he was with my mother when he became sick. Can you imagine having your two and three year old babies being intensely sick at the same time and hospitalized in different locations? I was overwhelmed. Najja's condition was scary for us because of the Sickle Cell Disease.

During her stay in the hospital, the doctors worked tirelessly to treat her for the virus. She was given lots of IV fluids and antibiotics to fight off any possible infections. She stayed in the hospital for seven days and then released. Her brother was treated and released after five days.

December 2000 is when she became sick again. This episode began one night after I had put her to bed. It was about 2:00 a.m. in the morning when she began to cry. I went to her room to see what was wrong. I found her cradled in the fetal position on her bed. I picked her up and asked her what was wrong. Through crying, she said, "my back and belly hurt bad." I asked her if it was the "bad" pain as she would call it. She said, "yes." I went to the bathroom grabbed a towel, one large enough to fit around her waist; I dampened it and warmed it in the microwave for about two minutes. I cooled it off a little and wrapped it around her waist in hopes the heat would soothe the pain. I grabbed her Motrin and gave her some. She cried for nearly 30 minutes and while I applied the hot compress. Eventually the pain stopped and she fell asleep. Seeing her relieved calmed me as well.

2001

Najja did not have any painful crises, viruses or hospitalizations for the next four months. It was April 8, 2001 and Najja woke up about 1:00 a.m. screaming furiously from pain in her back and stomach. Somehow these episodes seemed to surface at night and would happen immediately. I could tell the pain was intense because she screamed and clinched her stomach. This time I did not attempt to treat her at home because the screams were so intense I could see the pain her eyes. This was heart-wrenching and scary because she cried continually and the pain seemed unbearable. I began to cry as well; I could not bear to see her in such excruciating pain.

Expediently, I dressed Najja and we went to the hospital. Once we arrived, she was seen immediately and the doctor began to examine her. As with other visits, blood was drawn, urine was taken and she was given the IV. Even though the pain had subsided, she was given Tylenol with Codeine to help prevent another episode. For the next few hours I waited for her IV to finish and her lab results to come back. It took about five hours before she was released to go home.

In May 2001, Najja approached her 5th birthday, which was on May 29th. From birth I kept Najja home with her baby sitter Edmonde and did not enroll her into day care or any other school like setting because of the health issues. I did not want to risk her being exposed to any further illnesses. During her time at home, she had developed well on all levels. She grew at a normal rate and she had great vocabulary; she was outgoing and friendly. Even though she experienced a few hospitalizations, fevers and a few crises, she had not had any of the other symptoms of the disease. Little did I know, that was about to change.

A week after her 5th birthday, we had an appointment with her hematologist for a routine checkup. During the examination, a basic physical was done; her eyes, ears, and mouth were checked. Her limbs and her spleen were checked. The doctor asked a lot of questions about how she was doing on a daily basis. The doctor commented that Najja was lucky because she had not had any major illness outside of the fevers and a few pain episodes. She said by age five many children have had several transfusions, problems with their spleen or other health problems. I asked, "how can we tell what is happening inside Najja's body?" "How do we know if her internal organs are in good order?" She responded, "There are quite a few tests that Najja can take to check her internal organs."

She went to her desk and took out a sheet that listed several comprehensive tests. She called it a checklist. This list had a series of tests that were recommended for children with Sickle Cell Disease. Such tests included an eye exam, audio exam, dental exam, and endocrinology testing. The list also stated such tests as an MRA, MRI, cardiology tests, TCD (transcranial Doppler), urinalysis, and abdominal sonogram. I was not sure what some of these tests were, so I asked her to explain each of them to me.

As I reviewed the list, three of the tests captured my attention. These were the MRA, MRI and the Transcranial Doppler. I asked her to explain the purpose of each test. She explained that the MRA (Magnetic Resonance Angiograph) is a test that uses magnetic scan to look at the blood vessels in the body or on the brain. It is designed to detect problems within the blood vessels that may cause reduced blood flow or blockages to the brain or in the body. In many cases, it provides information that cannot be obtained by x-rays or CAT Scans. Next she explained the MRI (Magnetic Resonance Imaging) which is a test that provides clear information about the structure of the brain or the body. Basically, both tests are similar however, one shows the movement of blood within the veins and arteries (MRA) while the other test shows the actual structure of the brain or other parts of the body (MRI). She further explained the purpose of the Transcranial Doppler. This is a test that measures the velocity of blood flow through the brain. It helps to detect how fast or slow the blood moves through the blood vessels. She said these were important tests to get done because they could detect problems before they become life threatening or cause internal damage to organs.

Interrupting her, I asked, "What kind of damage can happen to the brain?" I did not realize that I opened myself up to a floodgate of anxiety with all my questions. She explained that many children with Sickle Cell Disease are prone to strokes. A stroke happens when blood vessels on the brain become blocked and cause insufficient oxygen and blood supply to the brain. She added, there are children as young as two years old who have had strokes. She stated, "Having a stroke is a very devastating occurence because the damage can be severe. Strokes cause weakness or numbness in the body; they can cause the body to be immobile while also causing a loss of vision, speech, and memory. Strokes are usually irreversible and can even cause death."

The next question was, "If I wanted Najja to take the MRA and the MRI where would I go?" She said that very few hospitals did these tests because they were very sensitive tests and not everyone could interpret them. However she recommended one location in Manhattan that had a fantastic neurology and radiology department; this hospital had the latest MRA and MRI equipment. Additionally the staff was exceptional with interpretation of the Transcranial Doppler (TCD) test. She recommended the Transcranial Doppler be taken first and depending on the results she would take the other two tests.

In my mind, these were the three tests I was interested in having Najja take. I took the information from her and went home to contemplate my next move. The next day, I called the hematologist and told her that I would like to set up an appointment for Najja to take the MRA, MRI and the Transcranial Doppler. She said she would get her secretary to set up the appointment. It took about two weeks to set up the appointment, get the referral from Najja's pediatrician and then get the test done.

The morning of the appointment, I dressed Najja and explained to her what was taking place; she had to have three tests done on her brain to make sure everything was okay. She asked why and I assured her nothing was wrong and these tests were simply precautionary measures so the doctors would know how to help her. On our way to the hospital, questions bombarded my mind. I was not sure what to expect. I felt nervous and concerned about the results of the examination.

We arrived at the hospital and went straight to the radiology department; the technician was waiting for us. He reviewed her paperwork and asked some routine questions. Next he told me she would take the Doppler first since it was simple.

For this test, she was placed on a small examination table which had an ultra-sound machine next to it. The technician took the transducer from the machine and applied a jelly-like solution to it and rubbed it along side her temples, above her eyes, and on the back of her neck. By doing this, he was able check the velocity or the speed at which the blood was flowing to her brain. According to the technician, normal blood flow ranges are under 160 to 200. If the number was higher than 200, the test indicated the blood flow was traveling too fast which would indicate there might be some kind of narrowing in the blood vessel.

After the Doppler was done, Najja was taken into another room for the MRA and MRI tests. These tests were done with her lying on a mobile bed that slid into a machine resembling a small tunnel. Before she went into the machine a head piece similar to a helmet was placed on her head; her ears were covered to lessen the loud noise from the machine. The technician instructed her to lie very still because any movement could give an incorrect reading and the results would be inaccurate. I asked him how long the tests would take and he said, "About 45 minutes to an hour because there are two tests." He suggested I remain in the room due to Najja's age, as it would help keep her calm. MRA and MRI machines are huge pieces of equipment and the experience can be quite frightening for first time patients.

As Najja took the test, she watched me to make sure I was still with her. I rubbed her leg and reassured her that she was doing great and the test would be over soon. When the tests were over, I asked the technician how long it would take for the results to be returned. "About a week," he replied. I thought to myself that a week wasn't too long. We thanked the technician and said good bye.

A week following the MRA, MRI and TCD, I scheduled an appointment at a Diagnostic Center for her to take the abdominal sonogram. The purpose of this test was to view her kidneys, stomach, liver, pancreas and spleen. Additionally, I scheduled an appointment for an echocardiogram with the cardiologist located at her birth hospital. Echocardiograms are designed to check the heart and how well it functions.

Three weeks after most of the tests were done, I made a followup call to Najja's hematologist to check on the results. Thankfully the abdominal sonogram showed no abnormalities; all of her organs functioned normally. The results from the MRA and MRI had not been returned but the doctor stated she would check further on those results and be in touch with me.

By now it was about July (2001) and I still had not heard from the hematologist in reference to the results from the MRA, MRI or the TCD. Although I was eager to know the results, I did not pursue the issue, I simply waited on their call.

One day I took Najja to the hospital to see a specialist. When I arrived to the specialist's office, I had forgotten the referral at home. I asked the office secretary what should I do. She said I should go back to the hematologist's office and request them to write another referral for me and bring it back to her so she could register Najja.

When I arrived at the hematologist's office, I explained that I had forgotten the referral and needed another so Najja could see the specialist. They agreed to my request and said they would prepare the referral right away. The clerk obtained Najja's chart to get her information. As she thumbed through the files, her phone rang and she stopped for a moment to answer it. In the meantime, she left the file open and I noticed that there were quite a few test results in Najja's file. At first I did not say anything because I did not know what to say. I just stood at the desk staring at the chart. Fortunately, she stepped away from her desk to speak to the doctor and I took the opportunity to read what was in Najja's file. It read, "six-year-old patient with condition known as stenosis of the carotid artery."

Though I did not know what the words meant, I read them again and I knew it was not good. When the clerk returned, I asked her to get the doctor because I needed to talk to her. When the doctor came, I pointed to the report from the chart and she began to read it. She looked at me and said she would be right back. She went into her office and closed her door. Within a few minutes, she came out, along with another doctor and the nurse. All three of them looked at me then one of the doctors said, "we need to meet with you immediately." I told them I could not meet with them right then because Najja had another appointment; I said, "I will come first thing in the morning." I left the office with an uneasy feeling because the look on the doctors' faces and the tones in their voices sounded serious.

Nevertheless, I took Najja to her appointment, and as I waited for them to call her name, various thoughts filled my mind. I wondered, "What on earth did they want to talk about? What could be wrong? Had they found something that would affect Najja's life in a negative way? Did she have some kind of terminal illness? Did she need surgery?" My mind spiraled out of control. I was so deep in thought I did not hear Najja's name being called until the third time.

The next morning, I woke up early and prayed; I had a feeling the news I was about to receive was not going to be pleasant. I prayed that God would give me the strength and wisdom to deal with what came my way that day.

I left my home and in about fifteen minutes arrived at the doctor's office. Upon arrival, I told the nurse I had a meeting with the doctors. She told me to wait a few minutes while she informed them I was there. The doctors came out and invited me into the conference room. As I sat down, the chief doctor began to explain why I needed to meet with them. She disclosed that the test results I saw showed some alarming results. They indicated there were some abnormalities in Najja's brain.

They explained that the MRA showed she had a condition known as stenosis of the carotid artery. It took me a moment to gather my thoughts then I asked them to discuss exactly what they were talking about. One of the doctors began to explain that the word stenosis means to narrow. The carotid artery carries blood from the heart to the brain. On the brain, it branches out into different arteries. One such artery is the anterior artery. This was the artery where Najja had most of the stenosis. The doctor said that the sickled cells were sticking to the walls of blood vessels causing it to narrow. As a result, blood flow and oxygen were not able to move through the artery freely. Consequently, over time the artery would narrow to a point where blood flow and oxygen would diminish significantly and Najja could have a stroke.

"How long do you think Najja has had the stenosis?" I asked. One of the doctors responded by saying she was not sure, since such an occurrence could have started at any time and progressed slowly. I wanted to know why she did not show any symptoms. The doctor stated, "symptoms vary and can go from mild to severe." Najja was what they referred to as asymptomatic. The doctors stressed that Najja was definitely at risk of having a stroke and I was told I should act immediately with treatment. I asked, "is there anyway to tell when she might have a stroke?" They said, they did not know, but it could be the next day, the next week or in six months. They just did not know. I was stunned.

Shocked and disappointed, particularly by their negligence to contact me regarding these results, I pointed out the tests were taken four months prior and I should have been notified. I could not make a decision at that moment. I told them that I needed time to digest all the information and discuss this with my husband.

Before leaving the office, I asked the doctors about the available treatments for the stenosis. They mentioned there were a few treatments available such as Transfusion Therapy, Hydroxyurea, and a Bone Marrow Transplant; however, the most common treatment was Transfusion Therapy. "What is Transfusion Therapy?" I asked. One of the doctors explained, "it is a treatment that raises the levels of normal hemoglobin in the blood and as a result lowers the amount of sickle hemoglobin." She further explained, "before the Transfusion Therapy begins, blood is drawn to get the correct blood type of the child. It is then matched with the transfused blood, which the hospital has on hand. The matching is important to prevent any problems during or after the transfusion." She explained, "the transfusion is administrated in the same way an IV is administered and it takes about one to four hours for the treatment to end depending on how much blood an individual needs."

She continued, "Once the treatment is over, most patients go home and for the next two to three weeks their risk for crises and other Sickle Cell related issues are lessened. After about two to three weeks, the transfused blood gets absorbed into the system and the sickled cells take over again. The child then has to be transfused again to raise the hemoglobin levels again."

I asked about the side effects of Transfusion Therapy. According to the doctors, Transfusion Therapy, over a period of time, can cause iron to build up in the body; too much iron can cause the patient to become sicker. Additionally too many transfusions can cause liver and kidney damage; however, there is medication to prevent the iron build up.

The second treatment the doctors mentioned is Hydroxyurea. It is a medication that was originally used to treat certain types of cancer. This medication has been on the market for approximately twenty years so there are no long term studies in reference to the side effects relative to the length of time used. Researchers have found it worked well with Sickle Cell patients by helping to reduce the frequent painful episodes and other symptoms of the disease. They explained that Hydroxyurea actually increases the fetal hemoglobin and lessens the chances of the red blood cells to sickle.

The doctors gave me more historical information about Hydroxyurea and its affects on Sickle Cell children and adults, hemoglobin levels and other pertinent information; they indicated this medication does not cure the illness but will help manage it.

I asked about the side effects of using Hydroxyurea. According to the doctors, the majority of children did not have any serious side effects. However some children have experienced nausea, vomiting or other stomach issues; yet most children tolerated the drug well. The dosage depends on weight and age.

The third treatment, Bone Marrow Transplant (BMT) is the most serious of the three treatments mentioned. This procedure is rarely done for numerous reasons: (1) Many individuals with Sickle Cell Disease do not have a donor match and therefore the treatment is not often recommended. (2) Some individuals have too many damaged organs and would not survive a procedure like a Bone Marrow Transplant. This procedure works best when children are young and their organs are healthy. (3) The procedure is costly and many insurance companies do not cover it.

The doctors explained that the Bone Marrow Transplant is a very complicated and serious procedure, which can cause death if the individual's body rejects the bone marrow. In order for a person to be considered for this procedure several criteria must be met: (1) the patient must have a matching donor (2) the recipient must be in good health and major organs must be functioning properly. Once these criteria are confirmed, blood work is drawn from the recipient and the donor and sent to a lab for DNA testing and other screening. If the results of the tests are favorable the process for the procedure can begin. The doctors further emphasized this procedure is high risk and should not be taken lightly.

After they finished educating me about the process, I asked them how long I had to make a decision and they informed me that I did not have much time. As previously mentioned, the results had been in her chart for quite some time so this news was distressing. I thanked them and said I had to discuss everything with my husband.

When I arrived home, I told Paul everything that had occurred and all of the information the doctors had given me concerning Najja's diagnosis. I explained that we had to meet with them immediately to determine which treatment would be best for Najja's condition.

The next day we met with the doctors; they gave my husband the same information they gave me but he advised them we wanted a second opinion and I agreed. This was a big decision and we wanted to make sure we were making the right one. Additionally, our faith in these doctors waivered as there was so much information they neglected to tell us. We advised them we would get back to them.

Once we arrived to the house, I called the hospital where Najja was born to speak to someone in the Hematology Department. I explained the situation and let them know I needed a second opinion concerning Najja's condition. The nurse made an appointment for one week later. During this time, I had become anxious and concerned, my mind was cluttered with numerous thoughts. I felt worried about Najja having a stroke.

On the day of the appointment, we dressed Najja and Justin and drove to the hospital. We went straight to the Hematology Department, registered and waited to be called. This appointment was not much different than the others as routine information concerning Najja's health status and her demographic data was taken. The head of the Hematology department met with us; I explained the purpose for our visit, showed her the results of the MRA, MRI and other tests performed and the options we were given. I told her that we wanted a second opinion. Before she could give her opinion on whether to place Najja on medication, she suggested we have the tests performed again. She also recommended an HLA test be done for both our children. HLA stands for Human Leuckocytes Antigen. The purpose of HLA was to see if Justin would be a matching donor for Najja just in case we considered the Bone Marrow Transplant as an available option. She told us once the results came back, she would call to discuss the information; she scheduled another appointment for a week later. After meeting with her, we felt more comfortable as she explained Najja was doing well compared to other children living with this illness. Additionally she scheduled an appointment with the Bone Marrow Transplant (BMT) department as we expressed our interest in speaking with them as well. Surprisingly, we were able to get the appointment for the following week. Her attentiveness and support encouraged us and calmed my uneasiness. Many questions flooded my mind so I knew I had to prepare myself for this next meeting.

Prayer gives me strength and in order to prepare for things to come I began to pray earnestly. I prayed for guidance and direction concerning what approach to take for my daughter's treatment. I prayed for emotional strength. I prayed for peace. Additionally I jotted all of my questions in a notebook: "What is a transplant?", "What would make someone a candidate for a transplant?", "What were the requirements for that individual?", "How was the Bone Marrow Transplant (BMT) procedure done?", "How long has this procedure been around?", "How often is this procedure done on children with Sickle Cell Disease?", "If this procedure was not done often, why not?", "What is the survival rate from this procedure?" Question after question, as they came to mind, I wrote them in my notebook.

One week after meeting with the hematologist she called and advised me the test results were back. She asked that we come in to discuss the results on the same day we were to meet with the transplant doctors, this was perfect. Even though I was still anxious about the outcome with chances being unfavorable, my hopes were high for normal results.

On the day of the meeting, we dressed the children and drove to Long Island where the hospital was located. My heart raced and anxiety crept in; imagine how I felt not knowing what to expect concerning my daughter's condition. We were invited to come in and wait for the doctor.

We waited for a while and three doctors came in, one was the attending physician. She held the test results in her hand and my heart began to beat faster. She went over the results and they were not as bad as my mind led me to believe. The Transcranial Doppler numbers were not as high as they were from the previous test. The number dropped from 225 to 170 which is considered normal range. Her opinion was that Najja was not at an immediate risk for having a stroke. Finally, the best news I had received in a long time! She stated it was important to have this test repeated in another year as things were subject to change. Next she discussed the results of the MRA and MRI which weren't as positive as I had hoped. The results confirmed Najja did have stenosis of the carotid artery, which meant she had hardening of the artery. The carotid artery is responsible for carrying blood from the heart to the brain. Once it reaches the brain, it branches out into different arteries, one being the anterior artery. Najja's complications were occurring in her right anterior artery. Sickled cells were sticking to the walls of the artery causing narrowing and the inability for blood to flow freely. She explained that the stenosis could not be fixed and the usual course of treatment for children with this condition was transfusions. She confirmed the results from the HLA test were good and Justin was a perfect match for his sister. We thanked her and left but had a two hour wait before the next appointment. I was more relaxed now and better prepared. As we waited for the next appointment I pulled out my list of questions and reviewed them. I wanted to be sure I did not forget anything once we met with the Bone Marrow Transplant doctors.

Finally three women came in. One was the head of the department, the other was a resident and the third was the social worker. We each introduced ourselves and I explained the purpose for our visit; we wanted more in depth information about Bone Marrow Transplants. Before the staff provided details about the procedure they wanted more history about Najja's illness. I provided a synopsis of how Sickle Cell had affected Najja, including details about her crises episodes and her Rotavirus illness; I provided complete details of all courses of treatments, hospitalizations, and tests performed on Najja prior to our visit with them. After reviewing the test result copies I provided for them, the doctors wanted to know about Najja's pre and post natal care. Recalling those painful memories, I shared my pre-term labor experience with them, including my diagnosis of Placenta previa. A complete history was provided to them concerning Najja's history with this debilitating disease.

The doctor explained, "A Bone Marrow Transplant is a highly-complicated procedure and tremendously risky on many levels. It is mostly used in cases where patients are experiencing severe Sickle Cell Disease complications such as repeated episodes of painful events, strokes and acute chest syndrome. It is usually used for children that are younger than 16 years old because the risk of organ damage becomes greater in older patients." She continued, "the patient's bone marrow which makes red blood cells with defective hemoglobin S is destroyed with high dosages of chemotherapy. The patient's bone marrow is then replaced with healthy bone marrow from a matching donor, usually a healthy brother or a sister. After the procedure, the donor's bone marrow begins to replace the recipient's bone marrow. If there are no complications or rejections, new cells restore the immune system and make normal red blood cells; the risk from this procedure should not be taken lightly. Complications include severe infections, bleeding on the brain, seizures and immune system problems." The doctor added, "if the patient's immune system is not weakened enough by the chemotherapy given before the transplant, it can attack the new cells and cause the transplant to fail. The patient may become infertile after the Bone Marrow Transplant because the chemotherapy destroys those cells and about 5% to 10% of bone marrow patients die."

The doctor confirmed Najja was a perfect candidate because she was young, her brother was a perfect match and her organs were in good condition.

As we were previously informed, the transplant was not a surgical procedure but similar to that of IV insertion. We were advised that pain medication is often administered as a remedy to the side effects of the chemotherapy. The medical team disclosed all the risks and complications associated with such a drastic procedure and after speaking quietly among themselves, advised us against the procedure as they did not feel Najja was sick enough to warrant such an extreme treatment. In their opinion, Najja was a basically a well child and did not require a Bone Marrow Transplant at this time.

Najja had another episode on October 14, 2001. She woke up at 2:00 a.m. screaming. It was more intense. I went into her room, picked her up and held her really tight. She told me, "Mommy it hurts, my back hurts!" Then I took her to my room and laid her on my bed. I gave her a teaspoonful of Tylenol with codeine and waited for the pain to stop. The pain returned the next day. She complained of pain throughout her body. She also had a fever of 101. I called her doctor and told her what was happening. She told me to give her some Motrin and lots of fluids. If the fever increased, I should bring her in. Over the next few hours I monitored the fever closely to see if it would lessen however, it maintain the same level. The next day, October 16, I decided to take her to the hospital because not only did she have the fever but she also began to complain of pain in her chest. When we arrived to the hospital, she was seen immediately. All the necessary screening was done and the decision was made to admit her.

For this admission, she stayed for two days and was released because her fever ceased and the results from her blood work were normal. The doctors indicated that Najja only had a mild crisis. The process of treating children with Sickle Cell is mentally and physically draining for the parents and the children.

Two months later she was hospitalized again on December 21, 2001. She started vomiting on a continuous basis; at least six hours. Additionally she had an ear infection which caused her to have a fever. I had no choice but to take her to the hospital where she was again hospitalized. This was the last episode she had for 2001.

2002

❧

Najja did well medically until February 15th. That morning, she woke up about 3:00 a.m. complaining of pain in her back. She said, "Mommy, my back hurts really bad," I climbed out of bed and went to get her Tylenol with Codeine. Before I could give her the medication, the pain worsened and the gut-wrenching screams began. I quickly gave her the medication hoping it would begin to take effect as quickly as possible. It was difficult to watch her go through these crises. I hated the cries, the intense excruciating pain and suffering she endured; I could not do anything fast enough to make the pain go away. Sometimes it seems as though the medication took forever to take effect. She cried so hard that finally she fell asleep. Not only was that relief for her but it was a big relief for me.

She had another crisis on March 15th. She was playing in her room when I heard her crying for me, "Mommy, mommy come, come mommy!" When I saw her, she was lying on the floor. I asked her what was wrong and she said her back and waist were hurting. I picked her up and consoled her. I began to rub her back and her waist. I hoped the pain would not get any worse and I immediately grabbed her medicine and gave her a spoonful. The unbearable pain lasted for approximately 45 minutes.

On April 21 she was hospitalized with a fever of 104.4 along with an ear infection. She stayed in the hospital four days and then released.

On June 7 the pain in her back and waist reoccurred. I gave her Tylenol and comforted her, waiting for the pain to stop. It wasn't always necessary for me to take her to the hospital because the pains would subside within an hour or two.

The month of July she did not have any pain; however, on August 16th another painful crisis happened. This pain was in her back and her waist. I gave her the Tylenol with codeine and she cried herself to sleep. On August 19th the pain returned; again in her back and waist. I thought to myself, "Here we go again!" I was so tired mentally of the reoccurring pain! I gave her the Tylenol and waited for the pain to stop.

On October 5, 2002 she had another painful episode; this time complaining of pain in her feet. I always comforted and massaged the aching areas of her body. Yet I had to be logical and think about what was necessary to bring relief to her suffering. I asked her to show me exactly where it hurt and she did. She pointed to the top of her feet around the toes and to her ankle. I massaged her toes and ankles then gave her Tylenol with Codeine. I wrapped her feet in a warm compress, which was a wet towel I heated in the microwave. I monitored the length of time this crisis lasted. After approximately 40 minutes the pain stopped and she was back to normal and playing.

By the end of October, we were ready for her to go for her annual comprehensive testing. My main concern was for her to repeat the previous tests: MRA, MRI,

Transcranial Doppler and abdominal sonogram. In addition to the recommended testing, Najja saw a cardiologist and eye doctor. Waiting for the test results always gave me anxiety. The cardiologist's report showed Najja's heart to be in good condition with the exception of a heart murmur. The results from all other tests were normal; I asked her to send a copy of the cardiology results to the hematologist and requested a copy for my records.

2003

It was January 2003, Najja was 6½ years old and having another crisis. We were home one Saturday morning, she had breakfast and as soon as she ate, she vomited. I gave her some ginger ale and she vomited again. I wasn't sure what else to give her, so I called my mother and told her what was happening. She said to boil some ginger and give it to her as a tea. I quickly took a piece of ginger from my fridge, mashed and boiled it. When it was ready, I gave it to her in small sips. She drank most of it, and seemed to be fine; (Ginger is a root that is great for any kind of stomach issues like stomach aches and nausea. I always keep it in my house). Within 30 minutes, however, she vomited again. I called her hematologist, since the ginger tea and ginger ale weren't working, and explained to her what was happening. She said if she vomited again I should take her to the emergency room. Before I could hang up she vomited again. I hung up the phone, dressed her and went to the emergency room hospital on Long Island. It turned out that she had a stomach virus. The doctors gave her IV fluids to avoid dehydration and eventually sent us home.

Another crisis affected her on February 3, 2003. She was in the day care center with me and as she played with the children she began to cry from pain in her back. I knew immediately that she was in crisis so I quickly grabbed her Tylenol and gave her two teaspoons. Within 20 minutes the pain was gone and she was up and bouncing around again.

By the middle of March, March 13th to be exact, she had another episode. It was a Wednesday night and she was getting ready for bed when she said, "Mommy my back is hurting." Before she could complete her words, she began to scream. She was sitting on her bed and she wrapped her hands around my neck and slipped into my arms. I sensed the pain she felt. She twisted in my arms and screamed, "Mommy, mommy, I can't take it! I can't take it! It hurts! It hurts!" I held her tight and told her I knew it hurt. I took her to my room, put her on my bed,laid next to her, held her close to my body and tried to comfort her. It did not help as the pain was raging a war in her body. I gave her two teaspoons of Tylenol with Codeine and also put a hot compress on her back. The pain continued and she cried endlessly. As a result, I began to cry. I wished the pain would just stop! I wished I could take it away. I prayed. I asked God to touch her and make the pain go away. I asked Him to ease the pain. She continued to cry until she fell asleep; she was exhausted. Finally she had some relief and she felt better.

The next day, March 14th, she woke up and was not in pain but she had a fever of 101. I called her hematologist. She advised me to give her some Motrin and take her temperature again within an hour. I did what she said but the fever was still 101 and continued for three days. On the fourth day, March 17th, I took her to see the doctor. She was examined and blood was drawn. The doctors were not sure why she had a fever so they gave her antibiotics and administered an IV and we spent a few hours in the day room. By late evening, we went home, however, we should have stayed at the hospital; we returned to the hospital the next day because she had a fever of 104. After examining Najja the doctor said she might have a viral infection and we should let it run its course. She continued to have a fever for the next four days before it went away. By March 21st she felt better.

On April 16th Najja woke up, ate breakfast and for most of the day she played with her younger brother Justin. By late evening and I took them both outside for a walk as it was a beautiful evening.The sun was setting and the wind blew mildly as we walked along our tree lined street. Suddenly Najja began to cry so I stooped down in front of her, put my hand around her waist and asked her what was the matter. She said her stomach was hurting. I told her to show me where and she touched the middle of her stomach. I followed through by rubbing it for her. I picked her up; walking as quickly as I could with them to get home. Once we arrived home, I put her on my bed and went to get her Tylenol and gave her the usual dosage. One of the great things about Najja was she took her medication without a fight and with ease regardless of the taste.

May 6th she had another episode despite our prayers that she would be better and pain free. Her 7th birthday was May 29th so we had high hopes for May being a better month. However on May 24 something new happened; Najja felt pain in her left eye. She said, "Mommy my left eye is hurting." I asked her if she had hit it or was she rubbing it? She said "no." I asked her if she was sure. She said "yes." I wasn't sure if this new pain was related to a crisis or something else. I called the hematologist and explained the issue. I told her Najja was experiencing pain in her left eye. She asked me if she had hit it or hurt it in anyway. I told her that I had asked Najja the same questions and she said "no." I explained to the doctor that the pain seemed severe because Najja was crying. She told me to give her the Tylenol and see if the pain would go away within the hour. The frequent pain subsided after a while allowing Najja to fall asleep.

Worry and anxiety came over me because I did not want the disease to affect her eyes; I had read a few pieces of literature which reported the disease could affect vision and cause blindness. Since this was something new, I thought it was important to monitor it so I began to write everything down in her journal. I found it helpful to keep an account of each incident or crisis along with details of each; additionally, the journal served as a reference guide when speaking with her doctors.

From May 25th to June 9th , she was pain and fever free which was good! It was a pleasure to see her pain-free, even for a little while. As her mother, I felt helpless to see her screaming with pain. This was really difficult. On June 10th the pain returned. It was midnight when I woke up to her crying. I was dismayed. I actually jumped out of my sleep and hurried to her room. I turned on her light to find her curled up in a fetal position calling for me. I held her in my arms and asked, "Where is the pain this time?" She did not respond because she was crying so hard. I said, "Mama, tell me where the pain is?" Through the crying she said, "My back, my feet" and then pointed to her hands also. I took a deep breath and immediately began rubbing her back. I called her father and asked him to hold her while I grabbed the medication. I knew by the way she cried the pain was severe. The cry was loud, deep and agonizing! My heart fell and my eyes filled with tears. I tried hard to be strong but sometimes I just couldn't! I just couldn't! Her dad attempted consoling her by massaging her feet, while I rubbed her hands. I gave her the medication and hoped the pain would just go away. "Just go away!" It took an hour before the medicine worked and she fell asleep.

After the June 10th crisis, she did not have another one until almost four months later, October 2, 2003. This period without pain was great! She went through the summer pain-free. I called these months "Our Sunshine Days." She did not have any hospitalizations or pain; she did not need any medication. Finally this was relief for all of us. She was strong and happy during this time.

October 2nd, she went to school and felt fine, however, by 11:30 a.m., I received a call from the principal that Najja was crying from pain in her left eye. She said the nurse had already given her the medication which I had left in school. I thanked her and told her I was on my way. The school nurse and the staff were already aware of Najja's condition; they were prepared to act whenever she became ill. At the beginning of each school year, I carefully briefed Najja's teachers about her condition. I made sure her principal and teachers were aware of how much water she needed, how much and what types of medication and I provided them with copies of her test results so they would know what to do in the event of an emergency. Additionally I provided them with literature concerning her illness.

After getting to the school, I walked as fast as I could to the principal's office. She immediately took me to the nurse's room where Najja was lying on a cot. She was crying terribly. I went over to her and hugged her. "Mommy, my eyes hurt!" she said. "I know," I replied, choking up with emotion, as I picked her up. The nurse helped me to put on her jacket and walked us out of the building. I took Najja home and put her to bed. By then the pain had subsided to a mild discomfort and eventually it stopped and she fell asleep.

October was the time of year I scheduled all of her routine appointments. I made a point of maintaining records of all test results; additionally I made sure I communicated with each of her doctors; even though a few of them thought I was "over the top" as a parent. My focus was keeping abreast of any changes in Najja's health, making sure I understood everything concerning her as well as linking her doctors together either by phone, fax or email.

Najja's doctors and I did not see eye to eye on the best course of treatment for her. They wanted to give her a transfusion, yet I was uncomfortable with this decision. As her mother and advocate, I needed to be certain she received treatment that was best; asking all necessary questions because I did not always agree with the doctors' decisions. I simply did not feel giving Najja a transfusion was the right answer.

2004

❧

January 2004 came and by then Najja was seven years and four months old. Though excited to welcome in the New Year, I was concerned about the uncertainty of her health. I pondered on the kind of year she would have. Mostly, I had concerns about her having a stroke. I would often feel nervous about her, yet remain strong and alert.

On January 9th, Najja came home from school and seemed fine. Just before she had dinner, however, she complained of having pain in her right eye. She was not crying, but she complained and whined about the pain. "What does the pain feel like?" I asked her. She said it felt like someone was punching her really hard with their fist in her eye. She then rested her head on my shoulder. I comforted her by rubbing her back and kissing her ear. She then asked me, "Why do I get sick so often?" "Why do I have pain?" She wanted to know if I felt the same type of pain, I told her, "no."

To answer her questions, I began by telling her that she knew she had Sickle Cell Disease which came from her dad and I possessing the Sickle Cell Trait. I told her everyone had cells in their bodies which enable them to live and those cells are shaped like donuts. When individuals have

Sickle Cell Trait, some of their cells are round and some are sickle-shaped. That was how some of her daddy's cells and some of my cells were shaped, I explained. I told her that she received all the sickled cells from us. Therefore, she has the disease. I further explained that inside her body, her cells have to move through her tiny blood vessels to carry oxygen to different parts of her body but because her cells were sickled, they clump together inside the blood vessels causing her blood flow to decrease. When there is insufficient blood flow and oxygen she will have pain. She then asked, "Mommy do yours and daddy's blood vessels get blocked? I told her "no" because only a small amount of our cells are sickled. We have more round blood cells which can move through our blood vessels much easier.

She asked if Justin had the disease also. I told her "no." I explained that her brother received all of the round cells. She responded, "Mommy it's not fair. I don't like this disease and I wish it would go away." I told her I wished it would go away too but advised her she may have to live with it for a long time until a cure was found. I advised her that she should always let us know when she has pain and reminded her that she has to take her medicine and drink a lot of water so she can feel better. I explained that the water prevents the cells from "sticking together" and will help her organs stay healthy. The conversation was difficult to have because I had to find the right words to help her understand.

I would have her drink about five 8 oz cups of water everyday. This was in addition to her juices and milk. I reminded her continuously how important it was to drink so that her cells would stay healthy. I also reminded her when she felt tired she must rest. Another thing I explained to her was the importance of eating healthy foods. I was big on that. I did not allow her to eat "junk" food. I gave her a lot of fresh fruits and vegetables. On a daily I would give her fruits such as red grapes, as they contained polyphenols which are antioxidants. Apples are a good source of pectin. Blueberries and raspberries are packed with nutrition; they are filled with fiber, minerals and vitamins and are loaded with antioxidants. These fruits have one of the highest antioxidant capacities which help the body combat cell damage while also increasing immunity against diseases. She would not willingly eat the blueberries and raspberries so I would blend them with apple juice and a little water, strain the liquid then give it to her to drink as juice. She ate lots of citrus fruits such as oranges, grapefruit and lemon which I would use to make lemonade. These fruits are full of vitamin C which is a strong antioxidant that promotes growth; citrus fruits also help maintain bones, skin and red blood cells. Other fruit such as bananas, pears and peaches made great snacks. She did not like to eat vegetables especially broccoli, cauliflower or Kale so I became creative with the preparation of her vegetables. Kale is rich in beta carotene along with vitamins A, C, and E; having more beta-carotene and vitamin C than other green vegetables. It is a good source of folic acid, which helps to prevent heart disease. It also contains calcium and magnesium, two minerals that are important for strong bones. It also contains lutein, which protects against mascular degeneration. She liked and ate a lot of carrots and spinach.

In order for her to receive the right amount of vegetables I made them into what I called "Green Soup." Vegetables like leeks (leeks contain folic acid, calcium, potassium and vitamin c), kale, spinach, carrots and turnips were blended into a homemade broth; I used chicken to make the broth and slightly steam the vegetables in it. Next I would blend the vegetables and the broth together into a creamy green soup. I gave her a cup with her lunch or dinner. At other times, I prepared the soup with pumpkin, sweet potatoes, carrots, lima beans and spinach. Sometimes I used mustard greens, sweet potatoes, white turnips and broccoli. Each week I chose different green vegetables to make her soup. Additionally I prepared most of Najja's juices, particularly fresh carrot juice. I combined various fruits and vegetables such as carrots, beets, celery, parsley, ginger and red apple to make the juice. Another juice was fresh spinach blended with Granny Smith apples; this juice was a good liver cleanser not only for Najja but the entire family. Najja's favorite was the pineapple and ginger juice. As mentioned previously, junk food was kept to a minimum – she did not eat many chips, cheese doodles, cookies or other such snack foods. Instead of dairy milk, regular eggs, and cane sugar I used soy milk, brown eggs, and brown sugar. She did not complain about the diet I placed her on because it was understood that she had to remain as healthy as possible.

2005

By January 2005 Najja turned nine years old. She had taken her yearly comprehensive test and I waited for the results. Due to my work schedule it was challenging to coordinate and make sure all of the doctors received the test results. Thankfully all of the results, including her vision tests were normal and she did not have Sickle Cell Retinopathy, which is a condition that occurs when the sickled red blood cells block the tiny blood vessels in the back the eyes. Her echocardiogram showed normal intracardiac anatomy. It showed mild mitral regurgitation which is a condition in which one of the heart valves allows small amounts of blood to leak backward into the heart; however, this was not a problem because Najja had good ventricular function. The Transcranial Doppler and MRA were the tests which concerned me most; the Transcranial doppler showed slightly higher velocity of blood flow to the brain and the MRA showed that Najja had new and progressive narrowing in the right anterior artery. The doctors were concerned about her being at risk for a stroke so they emphasized the importance of treatment.

Until May 16th Najja had done extremely well. We were on a flight to Florida for a trip to celebrate her birthday at

Nick Hotel for Kids. Halfway through the flight, she began to complain from a slight pain in her back. I rubbed it for her but it worsened in a matter of minutes and she began to cry. The unfortunate thing was I had left her medication in the check-on luggage by mistake and there was no way of getting it. All I could do was massage her back and hope that the pain would be short-lived. As she cried, one of the flight attendants came over to inquire as to why she was crying. I explained that she had Sickle Cell Disease and she was in a crisis. Immediately, the attendant told me she was also a massage therapist and she was trained in muscle relaxation. She started to massage her back. She also offered to give Najja a Tylenol. I accepted it and gave it to her with some water. The flight attendant also assured me that the flight would end in about another 30 minutes, but it seemed like forever. Najja continued to cry and I continued consoling her. I felt helpless and frustrated and I prayed that the pain would stop.

By the time the flight ended, the pain had eased enough and she stopped crying but it was clear she felt some discomfort. I thanked the flight attendant for her help. She wished us good luck and said good bye.

Once we had our bags, we quickly proceeded to the hotel where we checked in; I took Najja to our room so she could lay down and get some rest. She complained about feeling weak and having a stomach ache. I made her some ginger tea and just waited out the pain and suffering. We were on vacation and I felt so bad for her because she did not feel well. By late evening she felt better and began to have an amazing time with the other kids at the hotel. Yet two days later she had another crisis. This time it was in her left eye. The pain was so intense I had to call the EMS. Once they arrived, they examined her and decided to take her to the local hospital.

Once we arrived she was seen immediately and a series of blood work along with a physical examination was completed. The doctor had a number of questions for me. He first asked me how many transfusions she had. I told him none. He wanted to know if I was sure. I told him, I was positive. He said she was fortunate not to have had any transfusions. He continued to examine her and asked various other questions about her past history to see if he could figure out why she had pain in her eye. They decided to test the eye pressure to see if there was any increased pressure in her eyes from the sickling.

Once it was confirmed that the pressure in her eyes was normal, he decided to give her a low dose of Morphine to ease the pain. I did not want her to take such a strong medication but he thought it was best to administer it so she would feel better quickly. I reluctantly agreed. Within 20 minutes, the pain disappeared and we were ready to go back to the hotel and enjoy our vacation. Before we left the hospital, the doctor assured me he would send the results of her blood work and the eye pressure results to her hematologist; he said he would also place a phone call to her. I thanked him and we left. We returned to the hotel and committed to enjoy the rest of our vacation despite the complications.

It was May 30th when she experienced another crisis in her left eye. Instead of taking her to the hospital I gave her some Tylenol and called her hematologist. She expressed that Najja may be developing migraines. She asked for a description of the symptoms and events that occurred before the headaches came. Before the headaches Najja was usually fine, but during the pain she would see dots in front of her face, her vision would be blurred or she would feel nauseated. Given this information, the hematologist definitely thought the pain was coming from migraines. The severity of the pain varied from mild to intense and I would treat her with Tylenol and hot compresses. The next painful episode was July 31st, still in her left eye so I gave her the Tylenol with Codeine to help relieve the pain. August 30th she had another episode. She was in front of our home playing when I noticed she sat down on the step. She held her left eye and said it hurt. I checked her eye to see if she had gotten anything in it or if she had bruises or redness but there was nothing wrong outwardly. She cried with pain which let me know she was having a Sickle Cell Crisis. By this time in her life, she had learned to differentiate the pain of Sickle Cell and regular pain. When she had pain, I would ask, "Which pain do you think it is?" She would answer, "It's the hard one; the Sickle Cell one" or she would say, "it's regular pain." She expressed this pain was Sickle Cell crisis pain and I comforted her accordingly as I normally would.

Like Najja there are many children who live with Sickle Cell Disease and I was given the opportunity to speak with a few of their parents. In speaking to them it was revealed their children were usually in crises for days, or even weeks. I once met one particular family during one of Najja's admissions to the hospital; the mother shared that her teenage son had been in crisis for two weeks, consistently. As a result he had to be admitted. She told me that the pain was constant with no sign of relief. My heart went out to him. She also told me that he was ill most of the time and he rarely enjoyed his daily life or went to school as he would like.

There was a teenager who had a hip replacement; along with having his gall bladder and spleen removed.

Then I met a woman whose four year old daughter experienced a stroke at two years old and now had to receive transfusions for life. Yet another mother stated her son was always sick and she did not know what had been wrong with him, but he had been admitted four times that year. There was a young five year old boy whose mom stated, "my son was always sick; he had his spleen removed and he had frequent painful episodes. Additionally he had been transfused so much that he developed iron overload in his body." After hearing these stories, I realized Najja's case was not as severe.

2006

❦

This was another challenging year in which Najja had several episodes with left eye pain. Each time I simply comforted her using massage, hot towel compresses and Tylenol with Codeine if she wanted medicine. I called her doctor a few times but the doctor insisted that the eye pains were possibly due to migraines. I was not convinced entirely so she scheduled an appointment to discuss the pain in Najja's eye. She indicated that Sickle Cell Disease usually did not have isolated eye pain as a symptom. We discussed Najja's MRA and MRI results; the doctor showed me on the films where the narrowing existed and explained what could happen to Najja if total blockage occurred. The MRA indicated the stenosis had not changed, yet Najja was still at risk for having a stroke. She urged me to consider treatment but as I explained to her and the other doctors previously I was not comfortable with either treatment option and needed to research them further. The eye pain continued through the Spring, either in her left eye or right. By May 4th she had her seventh pain episode since the beginning of the year. We were visiting my mother and the pain caused Najja to stop playing but she did not feel as if she needed the medication (Tylenol with Codeine or Percocet), she just wanted a compress.

As a result of such episodes, over the years, I taught her that monitoring and managing her pain was important. I told her that some pain would be mild, some moderate and other pain intense. With each episode, she developed an ability to recognize the level of pain she experienced. For her age she had more fortitude and a level of resilience that many individuals much older than she did not have. For this I was thankful to God.

One day I sat down with her and began to discuss the eye pains. Curiousity led me to ask Najja what the pains were like; I asked her to describe her pain to me. At first she said she did not know. I asked, "Does it feel like someone is tapping on your eye?" She said, "no." I asked, "Does it feel like a pounding pain?" She said "no." She said, "It feels like someone is punching me really hard with their fist."

Vacation time, May 15th and Najja experienced another painful episode in her left eye. We were on the way to Florida, but she did not have any complications on the flight this time. However, she did once we reached the hotel. Immediately I gave her medication and the pain subsided within 30 minutes.

While waiting for Najja to feel better, I called Dr. Sadanandan to explain the episode and inquire if she thought the flight triggered the pain. She indicated that she did not think the pain was related to the flight; she thought Najja was experiencing migraine pain. I asked if she thought Najja needed oxygen on the return flight; I wondered if the high altitudes caused a lack of oxygen to flow. She explained that she did not think this was necessary but it was my choice and I could contact the airline and speak with a customer service representative. Before ending the conversation, she advised me to bring Najja to see her once we returned to New York. I stated I would because I wanted Najja to have a physical examination before traveling to Mexico at the end of June.

Once we returned to New York, I took Najja to see Dr. Sadanandan. The normal procedures were done: blood was drawn, urine sampled, height and weight were checked, eyes and ears examined. Dr. Sadanandan concluded that Najja was doing well but as far as the eye pains, she recommended that Najja should see a pediatric neurologist. Such a specialist could probably pinpoint why the eye pains were occurring so frequently. Upon hearing this, I agreed. Within a week, I was able to see the neurologist. During the visit he asked many questions about my pregnancy, Najja's delivery and her early development. I answered all of the questions easily because I kept a journal of my pregnancy and Najja's early development.

He asked numerous questions, including when the eye pain began, this was his main concern. I explained it began when she was approximately seven years old. He asked me to pinpoint the particular times she experienced the pain. To my recollection, the pain was random lasting anywhere from 20 minutes to 2 hours. Additionally I explained the intensity of the pain; it ranged from mild to excruciating. He inquired about her diet. Najja's diet consisted of mostly healthy foods; lots of fruits and vegetables, whole grains, fish and chicken, I explained.

Towards the end of the meeting, the neurologist gave me a chart to write down Najja's daily meal intake and the times when the pains came on. He stated I should return in about two months with Najja and the chart. I agreed, thanked him and left. As I left his office, I was not satisfied with him or his suggestions because I did not think he had any idea of what was happening with Najja. The fact was, Najja was having constant eye pain and I was not sure how charting her meal patterns were going to help to figure out the cause of the pain.

A day after the visit to the neurologist, Dr. Sadanandan called me to find out how the visit went. I told her it was just a routine question and answer session. I also told her that the neurologist asked me to chart Najja's daily meal intake in order to figure out if what she was eating had anything to do with the eye pains. Dr. Sadanandan thought charting the meals was a good idea because by doing so the neurologist could possibly rule out or factor in whether the foods she ate had anything to do with the eye pains. I told her I would definitely chart the meals and note the times the pain came. While Dr. Sadanandan was on the phone, I reminded her that we were leaving for Mexico within a few weeks and I would contact the medical division of the airlines to obtain the medical statement form. Once I received form, I would send it to her so that she could fill it out. She responded by saying she did not know why I insisted on getting oxygen for Najja. I acknowledged her concerns and I told her I would feel better if she would fill out the form so that I could get the paper work started.

Within a few days, I called the airline to get information on how to obtain the oxygen; as I spoke to the representative, I was told that the form could not be mailed however, I should go online to retrieve it. I should fill out the top portion then send it to the hematologist to complete the remainder of the form. The representative continued by saying that the hematologist would then fax it to the airline's medical department where they would review it and then send a decision to me. It would take seventy two hours to process the application and it would cost $100 for one liter of oxygen. Najja would need two liters; one liter for the departing flight and one liter for the returning flight. The whole process seemed fairly simple so I did not ask any additional questions.

May 29th was Najja's 10th birthday and we had traveled to North Carolina to celebrate with close friends and their children. Everyone seemed to be having a great time; sharing stories, playing games, skating, eating and listening to music. Najja played with another child at the party but then I noticed she stopped to rub her eye. She told me her eye was hurting again. I took her inside and gave her some Motrin and within 30 minutes she was up playing again.

The next day I called Dr. Sadanandan and told her about the eye pain. She insisted the pain sounded like a migraine; she advised me to give Najja her medication and allow her to rest until the pain subsided. She told me I could bring Najja in before we traveled to Mexico. Dr. Sadanandan was always available to assist; this was important for me.

A week after we returned to New York we met with Najja's doctor. The routine exam was completed and everything was normal with clearance for Najja to travel.

As the trip drew closer, I went to the airline website to retrieve the form. Once I obtained it, I looked it over and began to fill out my portion. I faxed it to Dr. Sadanandan's office so she could to fill out the section "to be completed by physician." Once she had completed her portion, she faxed it back to the airline to be reviewed. It took a week for the airline to respond to my request. I received a fax confirming approval of the request and all I had to do was pay the $200 for the oxygen. Immediately I made the payment.

On day of the trip, we arrived to the airport ahead of time in order to have enough time to check in and deal with any issues that may surface. During the check in, I asked the reservationist to check to make sure the oxygen was on the board. As she checked, she said, she did not see the request.

I explained to her that the paper work was done two weeks prior; I handed her copies of the approved request. She reviewed it and went back to the computer to research further. She found that the oxygen was ordered but it was placed on our connecting flight which was from Mexico City to Puerto Vallarta. The reservationist made several phone calls to get another liter of oxygen placed on our outbound flight. It took about 20 minutes to rectify the situation. However, the oxygen was on the aircraft and we were ready depart. This mistake also caused the flight to be delayed which caused me to be very upset.

The flight from New York to Mexico City was about 4 ½ hours. We connected to another one hour flight from Mexico City to Puerto Vallarta. During the first part of the flight, I told Najja that she would have to put on the oxygen mask once the plane had reached a high altitude. She agreed and an hour into the flight, I put the mask on her for about an hour. She could only take it off to drink a few cups of water to keep her hydrated.

The first three days in Mexico, Najja did well; she played in the pool for hours. She built sand castles and buried herself in the sand. She ran, jumped and basked in the sun. She had a fantastic time. Since the sun was extremely hot I reminded her to drink plenty of water. Additionally I made her wear a sun hat to help shield her.

On June 27th, the fourth day of our trip, she woke up with pain in her left eye. She cried moderately, so I gave her a dose of Motrin and hoped the pain would not worsen. We were in a foreign country and I was not aware of how their medical system worked; I wasn't sure if they knew anything about Sickle Cell Disease or how to treat it so I was concerned and hopeful that she would get better. The pain lasted for about two hours and she stayed in bed for most of that day. By late evening, she felt better and she did well for the remainder of the trip.

We returned from Mexico on July 2nd. Najja had tolerated the flight, without any problems. Of course I had the oxygen on hand in case she had needed it. She had used it for about an hour on both flights. Once we arrived home, I called Dr. Sadanandan and told her about the eye pain Najja had while we were away.

On July 13th, Najja woke up with a fever. After I took her temperature, the thermometer read 103.4 and she also complained of a sore throat. I gave her the Motrin and waited for about five hours, but the fever did not break. As a matter of fact, the fever lasted most of the day and her temperature basically remained the same. The following day, Friday July 14th, I called Dr. Sadanandan and told her that Najja had suffered a fever of 103 degrees for a day and a half. She asked me to bring her in as soon as I could.

I hung up the phone, and told Najja to get dressed because Dr.Sadanandan wanted to see her. So as quickly as she could, she dressed and we left for the hospital. As we walked in the office, Dr. Sadanandan concluded that Najja did not look well. She took Najja into the examination room and asked the nurse to complete routine bloodwork and urinalysis after she examined her. Najja was given Motrin to reduce her fever and an IV to keep her hydrated.

While we waited for the blood and urine results to be returned, Najja and I stayed in the day room. This day room was like a comfort zone for the children and their parents. It was actually built into the Hematology/Oncology Department. It was a big room with three or four beds, reclining chairs, three TVs and accompanying DVD players. One portion of the wall was lined with a shelf of videos, books, toys and games for all ages. It was set up for those children who came into the hospital because they didn't feel well. Such children were not sick enough to be admitted, but they needed some kind of treatment – whether it was medication for pain, transfusion, a basic check-up or monitoring for their illness.

The memories of being in this room in years past began to flood my mind. It was in this room I saw children being transfused; I met children and teenagers along with their mothers who had organs removed, received transfusions; kids who had experienced strokes and other Sickle Cell Disease related incidences. It was in this room where I shared my experiences and learned of the experiences of mothers who did not know what to do or how to care for their children.

July 24th Najja experienced a slight pain in her left eye but not as severe as previous times. However, we were in North Carolina for a mini vacation August 12th when she had another painful episode. This time the pain was intense causing her to cry for hours. Seeing her in this type of pain caused me to cry as well. My mother was with me and I asked her to get Najja's Motrin. Additionally I placed a warm compress over her eyes. A half hour passed before the medication took effect. She continued to cry intensely, mumbling through pain, "Mommy, please help me, Mommy, Mommy, please make the pain go away! I can't take it anymore, I feel like I am going to die!" I held her close to my chest and prayed. She continued crying until she was nearly breathless. The medicine did not seem to help so I decided to take her to the hospital. We arrived within ten minutes and went straight to the emergency room; she was seen immediately. I explained that she was in crisis. The doctor asked how long. I replied, "two hours." She was not crying as much by this time so there was no need to give her more medication;

I had already given her 400 mg of Motrin. The doctor asked about her medical history, how many times she had been transfused, and how many times she had been hospitalized. I explained that she had not received any transfusions but had been hospitalized numerous times for fevers, IV treatments and viruses. She was released after five hours.

The following morning I called her regular doctor, Dr. Sadanandan and explained what happened. She asked me to bring Najja in when we returned to New York. She expressed concern about the frequency of eye pain Najja experienced since January. She suggested I consider making an appointment with another neurologist and recommended one who practiced at a hospital in Park Slope (Brooklyn, New York).

September 27th Najja woke up with pain in her right eye. She did not cry but expressed discomfort. Najja was not the type of kid who liked to stay out of school. She is an amazing child, given the circumstances. She is filled with life and positive energy; she developed phenomenal coping skills during her young life. She was truly a trooper and would attend school even when she did not feel well. It is Najja's strength and drive that have kept me going through these years. As a parent of a child with a lifelong illness the child's determination is so helpful because it takes so much to care for him or her. Many times I found the process to be emotionally challenging as well as physically exhausting yet I continued to do everything possible to keep her healthy and ensure the best quality of life for her.

In October Dr. Sadanandan insisted I take Najja to the neurologist she recommended. This doctor is a pediatric neurologist and in Dr. Sadanandan's professional opinion she was thorough and well known in her field. She felt strongly that this doctor would be able to shed light on the cause of the eye pains. The appointment was scheduled for October 30th.

On the day of the appointment, I felt uncertain; not sure what to expect. Najja and I walked into the doctor's office and she introduced herself as Dr. S. She was pleasant yet straight forward. She asked to see Najja's previous test results and medical history. I handed her all of the documentation dated back to 2002, which is when Najja was first diagnosed with stenosis. She reviewed each report individually; she wanted to know if Najja was on Transfusion Therapy and if she had experienced dizziness, numbness in her limbs, seizures or blurred vision. I explained that she had experienced blurred vision and vomiting accompanied with her eye pain. Other than this Najja was fine. Additionally, I told her Dr. Sadanandan felt Najja may be developing migraines based on the symptoms.

We continued to talk and Dr. S indicated the stenosis seemed to progress since 2002. She pointed out the MRA in 2004 showed significant narrowing in Najja's right anterior carotid artery; according to her, the film showed early signs of Moyamoya Disease. I asked her to explain. Pausing, she explained as simply as she could, "Moyamoya Disease is an extremely rare disease in many parts of the world, except Japan." She explained the origin of the illness was not known and it mostly affected elderly people and young children. She described the illness as being a rare blood vessel disease in which a ring of blood vessels at the base of the brain progressively narrows. This narrowing causes blood flow to the brain to become restricted. Consequently, smaller blood vessels develop to compensate for the restricted blood vessel. Over time, the smaller vessels show signs of narrowing as well. Such smaller vessels curve, swell and appear cloudy.

Dr. S pointed out the disease could lead to irreversible blockage of the carotid arteries potentially causing ischemic attacks (mini strokes) leading to a major stroke in time. She stated the only course of treatment was surgery.

She was especially concerned though not sure whether Najja really had the disease. She wanted to reassess the stenosis as well as check further so she ordered some new tests to be conducted at her hospital. The radiology department called me later that afternoon with an appointment date which was a week later.

On the day of the test we arrived 20 minutes early as Najja was anxious about the MRA/MRI machine. She did not like the noises the machine made and expressed her fear. Before the test began, I explained Najja's discomfort to the technician and she advised me that most children do not like the machine. Many were sedated or coerced, but in Najja's case the technician took her to the room and showed her the machine, explaining the process and how the machine worked. She wanted her to become more comfortable so she had her lay on the bed and moved her in and out of the machine. The technician assured Najja, accommodated her concerns and let her know the machine was very safe; Najja was fearful that the machine would fail, fall on her and she would be trapped inside.

The test took approximately 30 minutes and Najja handled it well. The technician advised that we should receive the results within a week or so.

A week passed and I received a call from Dr. S. She explained to me the results were back and that they were not good. Based on the test, there was even more stenosis of the right anterior artery. The test showed diminished blood flow within the remainder of the anterior cerebral arteries. The films allowed her to see deep white matter, which was an indication the small blood vessels were being affected; Najja was having the ischemic attacks (mini strokes). Dr. S explained that over time this condition would worsen and Najja could have a major stroke, which would be a disaster for her. She asked for Dr. Sadanandan's and Dr. Sawicki's (pediatrician) numbers because she wanted to call them and discuss the results. The next day I received a call from Dr. Sadanandan and she asked to meet with us immediately. She indicated this was a serious situation so we went the following day. The same day, Dr. Sawicki called. She was also extremely concerned. She had spoken with Dr. S and the prognosis was not good. She stated, "the stenosis has worsened and it is time for Najja to receive some kind of treatment." She advised me to have Dr. Sadanandan send her a report. When we met with Dr. Sadanandan I asked her to explain the treatment options once again, as she had advised us of how serious this situation had become. Najja was more at risk of having a stroke. She explained the less invasive treatment was Hydroxyurea which forced the red blood cells to make fetal hemoglobin versus sickle hemoglobin. As a result, the frequency of painful crisis would be reduced. Additionally the need for blood transfusion would be reduced.

She explained that Hydroxyurea was developed to treat certain cancers, however, researchers had found it also helped with treating the symptoms of Sickle Cell Disease. I asked, "What affect does this drug have on the stenosis?" She replied, "none, as the damage to those arteries is irreversible. The main purpose of Hydroxyurea is to increase the normal red blood cells."

I also wanted to know the long-term effect of that treatment. "It was not known as yet," she said. The drug was relatively new, so at that time there was no way of telling the long-term effect. "How is it taken?" I asked. "It is a capsule that is taken every night," she said. "Depending on the body weight and age of the child, two capsules should be taken nightly." She added that before the medication is given, a series of blood tests had to be done. One was to test the liver function. Since the drug can damage the liver, monitoring of the liver function is done before and during the time the patient is on the drug.

Actually, every three to four months blood is drawn to monitor the liver function. My biggest concern was whether Najja would feel sick from this drug. She reassured me that from her past experience, some patients complained of stomach pains, vomiting or weakness; however, these were only temporary side effects.

The other concern I had was whether Najja could get cancer from taking this drug. She assured me that from her knowledge, the answer was no. "How long does she have to take it?" I asked. For her lifetime, she answered. At this response, I took a deep breath as a feeling of sadness came over me. My husband wanted to make sure he understood that Hydroxyurea would not treat the stenosis, it could only lessen the likelihood of her having a stroke, so he asked the question again.

We asked her to tell us about Transfusion Therapy. Like Hydroxyurea, Transfusion Therapy does not fix the stenosis or cure Sickle Cell Disease. However, it helps to lessen the painful crises and the symptoms of Sickle Cell Disease. It is a treatment that is given once every two to three weeks intravenously throughout an individual's life. Transfusion lessens the sickled cells so the patient's body has more normal red cells for a period of time. The problem with Transfusion Therapy is that it builds up toxins in the body and therefore can precipitate other health issues. For instance, it can affect the liver, causing it to become thin.

We did not spend much time talking about this treatment as an option, because it was not. We asked her to tell us about Bone Marrow Transplant; another option we had discussed in the past. This procedure was extreme and highly risky. It is only used as a last resort and many families didn't consider it because many children with Sickle Cell Disease did not have a qualifying donor match. She added that Najja's case was different because she had a perfect match and therefore half the battle was already won.

According to Dr, Sadanandan, Najja was a good candidate as she was still young; her organs were in good condition and she had a perfect donor. She suggested that if we wanted to consider the bone marrow, the best thing for us to do was to speak to a transplant team again at the hospital on Long Island. We agreed. She also suggested that Najja take another Transcranial Doppler again to measure the velocity of the blood flow.

Before we left her office, we assured her that we would decide on a treatment option and get back to her. In the meantime we would get in touch with the transplant team so that we could meet with them and discuss the possibility of a transplant. As we left her office, I thought about so many things all at once. I felt overwhelmed and uncertain.

The next day, I called the Transplant Department. The secretary who makes appointments answered. I told her about Najja's situation and that I wanted to meet with the doctors. She said she could not schedule an appointment at that time. However, she would talk with the doctors and get back to me. I agreed and hung up.

That same day my husband and I sat down to talk about the different options. For him it was cut and dry. The only practical option was the transplant as it would be a definite cure for the disease. He felt that the other treatments were only palliative, and to him that did not make any sense. As he spoke I listened carefully and tried my very best to understand his point of view. For me it was not so simple. Though I was not in agreement with the other treatments, I certainly had my doubts about the transplant procedure. It seemed so extreme and risky to me, but we were also dealing with an extreme and deadly disease. I told him that before I could commit to putting her through such a procedure, I needed to do more research.

About a week after I had made the initial phone call to the transplant department, the secretary called to let me know that she had scheduled an appointment for us to meet with the team. She asked that I fax all the written reports of the MRAs, MRIs, Transcranial Doppler and any other test results that would be helpful. She informed me that on the day of the meeting, I should also bring the originals with me.

On the day of the meeting, my husband and I drove to Long Island. I was a little nervous because I did not know what to expect and how the team would respond. This was our second meeting with them. The first meeting occurred when Najja was six years old when she was first diagnosed with the stenosis. At that time they felt that she was not sick enough to have the procedure which was a concern for this meeting.

When we arrived, the secretary accompanied us to a big conference room with a huge table and several chairs. Two doctors, a social worker and the child life specialist were already seated. They invited us to sit down, and I explained why we were there. I stated that we were back because we wanted them to review Najja's records again; we wanted to see if she would be a candidate for a transplant. I reminded them that the last time we were there Najja was not considered a candidate because she was not sick enough to warrant such a procedure. I pointed out that her situation had changed since then and she had developed stenosis of the carotid artery.

The doctors said that they had read all the reports and that the stenosis was very severe. They indicated a Bone Marrow Transplant was a very serious procedure and should only be performed on individuals who had no other options. In addition, all the organs of that individual must be in good condition. Based on the reports they had reviewed, they didn't think Najja should go through the procedure at that point because of the severity of the stenosis.

They further stated that they would have to present her case to the tumor board. The entire team would thoroughly review her case and then make a decision. "What problems would the stenosis cause?" I asked. They said, "with this kind of restriction, she would most likely have a brain hemorrhage. Such complications would be life threatening for her." I took a deep breath and looked at my husband. I think we both felt the same disappointment, but we understood their point of view.

Before the meeting ended, the head doctor suggested that we consider putting her on Hydroxyurea and Transfusion Therapy for one year to see if both treatments combined would help with the stenosis. I told them that we were in the midst of deciding on a treatment and we would be meeting with Dr. Sadanandan soon. We thanked them for their time as the meeting ended and we left.

Within a week, I received a call from Dr. Sadanandan. She wanted to let me know that she had received a report from the Tumor Board. It stated that Najja could not be a candidate for a transplant because of the right-sided supraclinoid carotid artery stenosis which had resulted in ischemia. This meant that the stenosis was so severe Najja was having mini strokes. Dr. Sadanandan further stated that the Tumor Board recommended Najja immediately start hypertransfusion and Hydroxyurea treatment and we should follow this up with a Transcranial Doppler every three months for one year to see if she showed any improvement in the velocity. If improvement was seen, she would be re-evaluated for the Bone Marrow Transplant.

I immediately asked Dr. Sadananndan to fax a copy of the report to me, so that I could read it myself. Once I received the report, I read it over and over again. What the report said was simply that the narrowing was too severe for her to go through a transplant. I was stunned and devastated. I just wanted something to work! I just wanted someone to help her!

That afternoon as my husband walked through the door I handed him the report. He read it and he was also disappointed. He handed it back to me and we both sat down at the kitchen table staring into space. Finally, he said we should get another opinion. I nodded my head in agreement, and told him I would call Dr. Sadanandan to discuss the matter with her.

The next day, I called Dr. Sadanandan. I told her we wanted a second opinion, just to hear what another doctor would say. She said there was another doctor she could refer us to. He was located at a hospital in Manhattan. His name was Dr. Del Toro and she would get his number for me and call me back.

It took about a week for her to call me back, but when she did she gave me the number and said Dr. Del Toro had transplanted a child with Sickle Cell Disease about three years ago and as far as she knew, the child had done well throughout the procedure. She indicated he may be able to assist.

October and November passed without Najja having any type of crisis. She experienced a mild crisis, left eye pain, on December 13th. The usual treatment of warm compress is what I gave her, along with her Motrin. Instead of driving her to school that day, we walked as a way to alleviate the stress we endured. She expressed how annoying the eye pains were for her and she wished the doctors could find a treatment for her. I assured her that the doctors were working on an option for her but it may take some time. She wanted a cure and I told her we must continue praying for one. Within a few minutes we reached her school; I kissed her and told her to have a good day. This was such an emotional time for each of us. As I walked back home, I cried because my heart went out to her. She seemed somber and worried and I felt helpless. I had to make a decision concerning her treatment.

Prayers for Guidance

❦

Stretched across the bed, I began to talk to God. "Lord, I need to talk to You. I need a sense of direction and some guidance as to where to turn and what to do. I need to find a solution. I know You can fix this because it says in your Word, "The things that are impossible with men are possible with You." I prayed throughout the entire journey as praying and trusting God had been the guiding force in our lives. I do not think we could have gotten this far without His divine power and intervention.

The next day, December 14th, Najja came home from school and as she sat on the couch she told me her left eye was hurting again and this time her vision was blurred. I told her to lie down and I made a hot compress to help soothe the pain. I waited for about fifteen minutes before I gave her any medication, but it didn't stop and seemed to worsen. So I gave her Motrin. Within half an hour, she vomited. I boiled some ginger tea and gave her a cup to drink just to calm her stomach. She soon fell asleep.

Six days later, December 20th, she was ill again, this time with something totally different. She had contracted a stomach virus. She was vomiting, had diarrhea and weakness in her body. She regurgitated everything I gave her and diarrhea followed. I called Dr. Sadanandan and told her I thought Najja had some kind of virus. I told her about the vomiting, diarrhea and weakness. She told me to give her plenty of fluids and try to bring her into the hospital so she could be checked out.

Immediately, I dressed her and we went to the day clinic. By the time we reached the clinic, she had developed a fever of 102 degrees. She was put in the day room for observation for about two hours. However, she was still vomiting so Dr. Sadanandan suggested she be admitted overnight for observation; I agreed. Upon admission, she was given an IV, to replace the fluids she had lost. She was also given Motrin for the fever and antibiotics to fight any possible infections. She remained in the hospital for two days.

2007

The new year brought many challenges although I was excited about newness. On January 5th Najja woke complaining of the pain in her left eye. I asked her, "How severe is the pain?" She said, "it is painful and it is pounding; as if someone is punching me in my eye." She rested for a while after I gave her some Motrin. The pain only lasted thirty minutes and she wanted to go to school. I advised her if it started again to let her teachers know and I would pick her up.

January 18th she experienced another episode; She woke up crying and complained of pain in her right eye. I gave her the usual treatment along with massaging her back, temples, around her eyes, her neck and the bottom of her feet attempting to bring her some comfort. By mid morning the pain had ceased but she had developed a fever, sore throat and chills.

I called Dr. Sadanandan and told her about Najja's symptoms. "How high is the fever?" she asked. I told her it was 101. "It sounds like a virus and you should consider bringing her into the clinic," she advised. I told her I would get her ready and bring her in. I started to get her ready as soon as I hung up. We were soon out the door and on our way to the hospital. Once we arrived, the nurse led her to the examination room and took her temperature. By that time the fever had spiked to 102. The nurse gave her Motrin. She also drew her blood, tested her oxygen level and collected her urine. The blood work and the specimen had to be sent to the lab; therefore we had to wait for the results which took about two hours.

While we waited, Dr. Sadanandan recommended Najja be given some IV fluids to replenish what she had lost. Within two hours, the blood and urine results came back and the numbers were normal. Her fever was down also, so Dr. Sadanandan decided to take her off the fluids and said we could go home with a prescription for antibiotics for her to take for a few days.

I was happy it wasn't one of those instances where she had to be admitted into the hospital because neither one of us liked staying in the hospital. She did not like being there because her sleep was constantly interrupted with medical staff checking her vital signs. The hospital was not our favorite place; there was not much to do except watch television; the interruptions of checking on her, cleaning staff and other distractions was equally as frustrating for me.

On March 5th Najja woke with a feeling of weakness. I asked her if she had any pain. She said, no but that she felt nauseated; within minutes she was vomiting. I thought she had an upset stomach, so I gave her some ginger tea and hoped that she would feel better in order to go to school. She did improve and was able to do so. About mid-day, I received a call from the principal. He stated that she was vomiting. I told the principal I would be there to pick her up. As I walked into the nurse's office, she was vomiting again and she looked very sick. When we arrived home, I called Dr. Sadanandan and told her that Najja had vomited three times within four hours. She asked if Najja had any pain. I told her no. She said based on the symptoms, Najja might have a stomach virus. She advised that I bring Najja into her office so that she could examine her to see the type of treatment she needed.

As we headed to the hospital, she complained that her left eye was hurting. Though she was not crying, I could tell that she felt some discomfort. She kept her eyes closed and had a frown on her face. It took about twenty minutes to get to Dr. Sadanandan's office. Once we arrived, we went into the treatment room where the nurse took her height, weight, oxygen level and temperature. Her temperature was 101, so she was given a dose of Motrin for the pain and fever. She was also given IV fluids to prevent dehydration.

By late afternoon, the fever had broken and Najja seemed to feel better. She certainly looked better, so Dr. Sadanandan gave us the green light to go home. She advised me to give Najja lots of clear fluids such as apple juice, ginger ale, and water. Additionally she said Najja should stay in bed and rest to allow the virus to run its course. She was released and I took her home where we sat down together and prayed.

On the morning of March 29th, Najja went to school and was fine when she left home. Nevertheless by mid-day, I received a call from her teacher saying she had a fever. She did not know how high it was as they did not have a thermometer. Immediately I rushed over to pick her up. When I arrived she was burning up. She also complained of a sore throat. After going inside, I took her temperature and it was almost 103. I quickly gave her Motrin and made a salt water and vinegar solution so that she could rinse her throat. She could hardly stand because she was so weak. When she was finished, I made her lie on my bed and I made a cold compress for her forehead. I called Dr. Sadanandan and explained that Najja had a fever of 103 along with a sore throat. Dr. Sadanandan told me to bring her in immediately. As I helped Najja get dressed, I noticed she had a red rash down her back. I checked her legs and it was there also. By the time we arrived to the hospital, the rash had spread to her arms and neck. She was taken to the examination room for a routine checkup where blood work was drawn. Dr. Sadanandan and another doctor began to speculate as to what they thought caused the rash and high fever. At first they felt that she had an allergic reaction to something. They wanted to know if she had eaten anything different from what she normally ate.

The other doctor suggested it might have been scarlet fever, but that would be very rare. They could not say for sure until the blood results came back. The decision was made to admit her. After her admission, many tests were done on her to determine why the fever would not break and why she had the rash. Each time the fever went down, it would return. She was given three different antibiotics; a bone scan was done and still the fever lingered. Finally, the disease control doctors were called in to examine her and analyze what would cause such a rash and the incessant fever.

By then it was April 3rd Dr. Sadanandan and the other team of doctors concluded that Najja had contracted some kind of bacterial infection associated with strep throat; this strand of bacteria was so strong they had a hard time finding an antibiotic that could get rid of it. Finally on April 5th she was given an antibiotic called Vancomycin, which happens to be a very strong antibiotic; within the next two days, the fever decreased and the rash started to disappear. The rash had covered her entire body like new skin. It was scary because it caused her skin to turn dark.

By April 10th, she felt much better. The rash had disappeared. The fever and sore throat were gone. Since Najja felt better the doctors decided that she should be released from the hospital and spend the remaining recovery time at home. This was good news for all of us. I was happy and relieved and Najja was eager to go home.

Najja's doctors cautioned me that her activities should be limited during her recovery period at home. She was not allowed to go school for the next two weeks which was fine with me because I really wanted to give her body time to regain its strength.

Over the next two weeks, my mother stepped in with her homemade remedies. She gave Najja fish soup on a daily basis. She would get the small sized fish and boil them into a broth. She added vegetables (carrots, pumpkin, sweet potatoes, fresh garlic, thyme and scallions. From this she made fish soup. According to her the fish soup would strengthen Najja's immune system).

Apart from fish soup, my mom also gave Najja pear leaf tea, another remedy to help strengthen her system. Of course there was the famous chicken soup with Irish moss. The Irish moss is a plant life from the sea and according to my mom it is great in strengthening the body.

Over the next two weeks while Najja was at home after being released from the hospital, she began to regain her strength and began to feel better. The fever, sore throat and rash had fully disappeared and she was ready to go back to school and resume her normal life. By then it was April 23rd and she was indeed ready for school.

On May 15, my husband and I went to see Dr. Sadanandan because she wanted to find out if we had made a decision as to which treatment to put Najja on. As we talked, she was very concerned and she made it clear that we did not have time to waste; too much time had already passed and we were putting Najja at risk by delaying. I told her that was not our intention and that we had decided to put her on Hydroxyurea.

Dr. Sadanandan did not understand why we were so reluctant to try Hydroxyurea treatment. She said many children were on the treatment and they were doing well. She stated that it would do more good than harm and assured us that Najja would be fine. Additionally, she would start Najja on the smallest dosage and see how she tolerated it. She said the most that may happen was that she would probably throw up or get a stomach ache.

Dr. Sadanandan indicated that before Najja took the medication she would have to take a blood test to see what her baseline liver function was and within three months the same blood test would be repeated to see if any changes had occurred. We agreed to this and set a date as to when we would bring her in for the blood test and the first treatment. That date was June 15th.

On the day of the appointment, my husband and I sat with Dr. Sadanandan and she reviewed with us how to administer the medication. She said we should give Najja one capsule with juice or water just before she went to bed. Then we should monitor her for about ten to fifteen minutes for any allergic reaction. We agreed, took the medication and went home.

After we reached home, I felt somewhat unsettled because in my heart I really did not want to give her the medication. But at this point in time, I did not have any choice.

That evening, I sat down with Najja and explained to her what was about to happen. I told her because of the narrowing in one of the blood vessels on her brain, Dr. Sadanandan and her other doctors were very concerned about her health.

They did not want the narrowing to worsen because it would make her get very sick. I told her in order to prevent some of the painful crisis and the eye pains, her doctors wanted her to take a medication called Hydroxyurea which is supposed to help produce more fetal hemoglobin. She asked, "what is that?" I explained that we are born with fetal hemoglobin, however within a few months of life, it decreases and our normal hemoglobin kicks in.

I explained in her case the sickled cells were causing problems in her body, particularly in the blood vessels on her brain; so the doctors have to try to stop the problems from becoming worse. She wanted to know if the Hydroxyurea would cure her Sickle Cell Disease. I told her no, it could not cure it, however, it would help decrease the chances of a stroke and the other painful crises. Her next question was if she had to take the capsule every night. I told her yes. She asked, "how long will I have to take the capsule?" I told her for a long time or until doctors and researchers find a cure for the disease. She sighed and I caressed her cheek. I further explained that she might get a stomach ache or vomit after taking the capsule, but apart from those effects, she should be fine.

Just before she went to bed, I gave her the capsule with a glass of water. I waited by her bedside for about twenty minutes just to see if she would have any reaction to it, but she didn't. Just to be sure she was OK, I asked her how she was doing. "Fine mommy, I am fine," she replied. I was happy about that. I kissed her, pulled the covers over her and said good night.

The next morning, when she woke up, she rushed from her room into the bathroom and threw up. She also complained of a stomach ache. Actually she was crying and could barely stand. I asked her if she was having a Sickle

Cell pain or a tummy ache. She was not sure, she said. I asked her to describe the pain to me. Normally if it was a Sickle Cell pain, she would describe it as if someone had punched her in the stomach. If it was just a stomach ache, she would say it was just pain.

I made her lie on the couch and I began to massage her tummy, while still trying to get her to give me more information about what the pain felt like. She still could not describe it. All she kept saying, as she cried, was "Mommy, it hurts." I grabbed the ginger from the fridge, mashed up a couple of pieces and boiled them in a pot of water. Within 15 minutes, the tea was ready. I poured it into a cup, added a tea spoon of sugar and tried to get her to sip it while it was hot. By this time, her cry intensified. I was not sure what to do at this point so I continued rubbing her stomach and while coaxing her to sip the ginger tea.

The disappointing thing about that day was, it was her graduation from 5th grade and she was really looking forward to going. By that time, it was about 11:30 a.m. and she was supposed to be at the ceremony by 1:00 p.m. It didn't seem as if she could go, because the pain did not cease.

I called Dr. Sadanandan and told her exactly what had happened. She wanted to know if Najja had a fever. I told her no, and I explained that she only had stomach pain and vomiting. I asked her if she thought it was the effects of the Hydroxyurea. She was not sure, as anything could trigger a stomach ache. I told her I would continue to monitor her and if it worsened, I would call her back.

As I ended the call, Najja called me and said her tummy was starting to feel a little better. "Are you sure?" I asked. "Yes," she said. I gave her the rest of the tea and asked her if she felt up to going to the graduation ceremony and she said "yes." She looked and felt much better so she dressed to go to the ceremony. Once we were all ready, we were on our way to see her graduate from 5th grade. The ceremony lasted about two hours and she did well the entire time. After it ended, we all went out to dinner and had a great time.

On June 20th, we had an appointment to see Dr. Del Toro. The purpose of that visit was to determine whether or not Najja was a good Bone Marrow Transplant candidate. He did not know that we wanted a second opinion as we were concerned parents simply seeking advice.

We introduced ourselves and I liked him instantly. He was friendly, pleasant and gentle. He invited us into his office and as we sat down, I began to explain why we were there. I gave him Najja's medical history from birth to present. I handed him the latest MRA and the results from the Transcranial Doppler. He looked them over for a few minutes and then excused himself from the room.

He returned after approximately ten minutes. He looked at us with an extremely concerned look in his eyes. It appeared as if he was trying to figure out what to say to us. From the expression on his face we knew what he was about to say was not good.

Finally, he began to explain, "According to the MRA and the Doppler results, transplanting Najja at this time is not possible. This is because the stenosis is too severe. With such severity, she would be at risk of hemorrhaging on the brain and therefore she would not make it through the transplant."

Like the other doctors from the hospital on Long Island, he explained that a transplant was a highly-risky and intense procedure. "If she were to go through such a procedure she must be in good health," he said. Once the transplant began there was no turning back, so her organs must be in good condition. I asked him to explain once again how the procedure is done.

Dr. Del Toro made it clear that a Bone Marrow Transplant was not surgery. He said it is a procedure that is long and intense. He stressed that it is a very serious procedure and it could take up to fifty-five days from start to finish. The first thing was that a matching donor had to be identified. He noted that one of the hardest hurdles was finding such a donor. In Najja's case this was not a concern because she had a donor.

Dr. Del Toro continued by pointing out that African Americans had only a 14% chance of finding a complete matching donor. He said that this was one of the reasons why the Bone Marrow Transplant procedure was not done as often for individuals with Sickle Cell Disease. He then stated after a donor was identified, a series of blood tests and physical examinations would have to be done on Najja and her donor.

Once these tests were done and the results were favorable, Najja would be admitted to the hospital to start the pre-conditioning procedures. After admission, she would have a surgical procedure done to place a central line in the left side of her chest right above her breast. The line would be the central point where all the medications and chemotherapies would be given through. That would be the same line through which the bone marrow would be given. Blood would also be drawn via the same line. Once the line had been placed, the next day she would be given the first dose of chemotherapy called Busulfan. This chemo would wipe out her bone marrow.

Dr. Del Toro explained that Najja would get this chemo for four days. Then after the four days, she would have one day of rest and then she would be given two other chemotherapies known as ATG (rabbit anti-thymocyte – globulin) and Cyclophophamide. These medications would keep her immune system suppressed so that the transplanted cells would not be rejected. Once her immune system was significantly suppressed, she would be given her donor's bone marrow through the IV.

Dr. Del Toro continued to tell us that the bone marrow procedure was not painful but the chemotherapies could damage Najja's vital organs such as her kidneys, liver and respiratory system. He also noted that the chemotherapies would make her sterile. In addition, he made it clear that the medications would make her feel very sick most days. She would be weak and she would not eat much or not eat at all. He also added that because of the stenosis, she could have a stroke. He stated there would be a waiting period of four to six weeks to determine whether her body would accept or reject the bone marrow. If her body accepted she would be half way out of the woods; however if her body rejected the bone marrow she could develop Graft versus Host Disease which is a condition that occurs when the recipient's body rejects the donor's bone marrow. There are medications for such a disease however if the medications did not work, the disease could be fatal.

Carefully I listened as Dr. Del Toro spoke. He said, the most dangerous part of the transplant was waiting for the new marrow to grow; Najja's immune system would be highly compromised afterwards. She would be susceptible to all kinds of infection and complications. Since her body would not be able to fight off any infection during that point, she could become very ill and even die. The doctor continued to explain that if her body accepted the bone marrow, which was a 80% chance, she could spend up to 55 days in the hospital for recovery. Once she was doing well she would be able to go home. She would have to stay home for the entire school year until her immune system returned to normal. She would need careful monitoring and special care, including weekly visits to the clinic. Added to this our home would have to be extremely sterile and she would only have contact with the people living inside our home.

I interrupted him to ask, "What could be done about the stenosis?" He said there was nothing he could do because the vessels were already damaged. However he said there was a great pediatric neurosurgeon that he knew at another hospital. His name was Dr. A and he was an expert in treating children with stenosis and Moyamoya Disease. He mentioned he thought it would be a good idea to meet with Dr. A to discuss Najja's situation. If he was willing to do the surgery and it was successful, then he would be happy to perform the transplant.

He told us not to worry as Najja was a strong child and the majority of her organs were in good condition and she was still young. He was almost sure that Dr. A would be able to help us.

Before we left his office, he handed us a book that we could read in order to learn more about the transplant and what to expect. He also gave us a second book for Najja, written specifically for children.

Dr. Del Toro introduced us to a young woman whose five year old son had Sickle Cell Disease. He had received the Bone Marrow Transplant. She was a parent advisor at the hospital and her job was to share with new parents the process of the transplant and her experience with it. We were very glad to meet her. She was definitely someone I would be interested in talking with; therefore, we exchanged numbers and we left.

The following day, I called Dr. A and was able to set up an appointment to meet with him. I was able to speak to him directly and not his assistant or secretary, which was a plus. He asked that we bring in all of Najja's MRAs, MRI and Doppler results.

The appointment was scheduled for the next two weeks. The day before the meeting, I explained to Najja that we were going to see another doctor to see if he could help treat the stenosis and the constant eye pain. She wanted to know what he was going to do. I explained that I was not sure hence the reason we were going to talk with him.

The day of the meeting came and all three of us walked into Dr. A's office and introduced ourselves. I liked him immediately because he was welcoming and courteous. I explained to him why we were there. I told him that Najja had Sickle Cell Disease and that over the past 11 years she had been hospitalized due to fevers, viruses and some short lived crises. In addition, she had been diagnosed with stenosis of the carotid artery. The stenosis had worsened to a point where she might be developing Moyamoya Disease, I added. I also told Dr A that we met with Dr. Del Toro to see if Najja would be a candidate for a Bone Marrow Transplant. I explained, according to most of her doctors the severity of the stenosis prevented them from agreeing to do the procedure and as a result we were referred to him. He asked to see the test results. While viewing them on his x-ray screen he showed us where the stenosis was located. He added that though the artery was not totally blocked, it was quite severe and she was at a high risk of having a stroke.

He further indicated that her brain had compensated for this by creating smaller blood vessels so that it could continue to get sufficient oxygen and blood flow; however, the sickling had started to affect the smaller vessels and they were beginning to show signs of narrowing. He pointed to some of the small blood vessels on the screen and explained that because of the narrowing, they were beginning to puff up and give off a cloudy appearance. The cloudy appearance and the narrowing was known as Moyamoya Disease. He said that the disease is very rare in most parts of the world except Japan and it mostly affects elderly people and sometimes young children. In children, the disease leads to seizures and sometime strokes. In Najja's case, the Moyamoya seemed to be progressing and this was probably the reason why she was having the migraine like headaches. She was not getting sufficient oxygen and blood flow to the brain and as a result she was having mini strokes which over time could cause bleeding on the brain, or a very devastating stroke.

Dr. A added that there were no treatments for Moyamoya Disease other than surgery. The procedure that is performed to correct this disease is called EDAS (Encephaloduroarteriosynangiosis): Encephalo means brain, Dura means membrane, Arterio means blood and Synangiosis means the regeneration of blood vessel. This procedure takes about three to four hours to perform and its main purpose is to create a new path so that oxygen and blood could sufficiently reach the brain. Better blood flow and oxygen to the brain would lessen her chance of having a stroke and would more than likely end the eye pain and migraine like symptoms.

I asked him how many surgeries of this type he had performed and what was the survival rate. He told me that he had done six surgeries and all of the patients were children who survived. "How many of the children had Sickle Cell Disease?" I asked. "Three of them had Sickle Cell Disease and the other three only had Moyamoya Disease," he stated.

"What were the side effects?" I inquired. He assured us that all surgery had risks, from the simplest to the most complex. This one was no different. This surgery could cause bleeding on the brain which could result in a coma or sensory loss. He said that Najja could get an infection, have a reaction to the anesthesia and there was a possibility that the blood vessels would not grow.

My other question to Dr. A was whether he considered the procedure complicated to perform. He said, "No. It may sound complicated but it is not, it is fairly simple." All he would do is take the external vessel from outside the skull and place it on top of the brain. I also asked him if Najja had to be transfused before and during the surgery. He said she would definitely have to be transfused before the surgery so that she would not go into respiratory failure from being under anesthesia so long. He informed me that Najja's hematologist would take care of that part of the procedure. I also wanted to know what the length of the scar would be. He replied by saying that it would be about three to four inches and that the area would be shaved before the incision was made. He also added that her hair would not grow back in the area again once the incision healed.

During the conversation with Dr. A, Najja was sitting on her father's lap taking in every word. Normally, she would have been very talkative and would have had her own questions to ask, but this time she was quiet. It was at that point Dr. A. asked that she sit outside of the room as he had noticed that she was becoming somber. When she left, he explained that he did not think she needed to hear all that information and it would only cause her to worry. We agreed.

Dr. A then stated that the surgery would be of more benefit to her because the stenosis would only get worse and at that point a stroke was inevitable and when it happens, it would be devastating to her. She could have serious brain damage which could lead to loss of speech, blindness, loss of muscle control and it would not be good. Dr. A made it clear that we should not waste any time in making a decision. I asked him how soon he would be able to do the surgery. He replied immediately. All we had to do was fill out the paper work so that it could be sent to the insurance company for approval. Once the approval came through, he would be ready to proceed. We agreed to get the paper work started.

Though we were extremely worried and overwhelmed due to the information we received, it was a pleasure to have met and talked with Dr. A. We had a wealth of information. We gained more insight about Moyamoya Disease and how it affected children with Sickle Cell Disease. We also learned more about EDAS procedure and how it would benefit children with Sickle Cell Disease. Again Dr. A. was great. According to him he and his team of doctors were one of the first to publish a paper on Moyamoya Disease.

Later Najja wanted to know why she was not allowed to stay in the meeting. I explained that Dr. A thought much of the information was overwhelming for her. The purpose of the meeting was to find out how the stenosis on her brain could be treated and if treatable the risk of her having a stroke would be reduced. She asked if she were going to die. I told her I did not think she would. Dr. A. had assured us that she would be safe and all would be well during the procedure. Reassuringly, I advised her of the same and reminded her that she was a gift from God.

Two days passed before I heard from Dr. A's office. When I received the phone call, it was from his secretary. The news was not good. She said there was a problem with the insurance company. She said that they turned down the claim because Dr. A. was an out of network physician and the insurance company did not pay for out of network providers. She said we would have to search for another doctor to do the procedure. I asked her if there was any way that we could get insurance company to accept Dr. A. She said she did not know. She said we would have to speak to the insurance company ourselves. I thanked her for the phone call and hung up. I was so disappointed. To me this was a road block.

My next step was calling the claims management department at the insurance company. The claims manager explained that it is not policy for the insurance company to cover claims from out of network physicians and there was not much we would do to reverse their decision. She gave me the name of another pediatric neurosurgeon who treats children with Moyamoya Disease. She advised that she would contact medical management to schedule an appointment with this doctor.

Within a few days, the insurance company called back to give me the doctor's name and the location of the hospital, which was in the Bronx. I was assured by the woman on the phone that this doctor was a phenomenal doctor and the hospital had a great reputation. She mentioned that she had scheduled an appointment for us to meet with the doctor for the next week.

The day of the appointment came; Najja, her dad and I went to meet with the doctor. The drive from Brooklyn to the Bronx was long. However, when we arrived at the hospital, I felt uneasy and was not sure why. Nevertheless, we walked into the doctor's office and was told by his secretary to have a seat in the waiting room. Within a few minutes, the doctor came out to greet us and invited us into his office.

Upon meeting the doctor, I instantly became depressed. Unlike Dr. A at the other hospital, the doctor almost appeared unwelcoming and he did not smile. We sat down and I explained why we were there. I told him about Najja's history and the problem she had with the stenosis, which had developed into Moyamoya Disease. I explained we had selected another neurosurgeon to do the procedure, however our claim was rejected by the insurance company. As a result, we were referred to him.

As a means of confirming the other doctor's assessments I asked him (Dr. G) to explain Moyamoya Disease and asked him the same questions I had posed to Dr. A. He gave us all of the details Dr. A had given us and thoroughly explained the procedure to treat the illness, the full process and other details associated with this condition. He indicated that the surgical team would include himself, the anesthesiologist, two additional neurosurgeons and a nurse. We wanted to know the side effects, he gave us the same information Dr. A had given us. The difference for this meeting is that Najja remained in the room and this time she asked the boldest and most alarming question either of us had asked. She wanted to know if she could die. Stunned, Dr. G., my husband and I looked at each other. He told her no and she would be fine. She breathed a sigh of relief. I then asked, "How will you be able to tell if she is getting sufficient oxygen?" He explained that she would be connected to many machines monitoring her vital signs, including an oxysimitor on her finger.

Dr. G's initial demeanor did not seem so "cut and dry" after our meeting. He answered all of our questions including confirming that Najja would not need a transfusion after the surgery. I asked, "What will happen after the surgery is completed and how long will it take for us to see her?" He said that we could only see her one at a time in the recovery room then she would be moved to the ICU (Intensive Care Unit) for approximately two days. She would remain under observation and then moved to a regular room as long as she continued to improve. He explained the EDAS procedure was only done by five physicians in the country yet it was a fairly simple procedure he had been doing for many years. Finally I asked if he could refer us to a parent whose child had received the surgery. Without hesitation he said, "yes." He stated, he had performed the same procedure about nine months ago on a boy around Najja's age. His Moyamoya Disease had been far more progressive than Najja's and he was doing well. He told us that he knew it was a lot of information and there was a lot to think about, but we should not wait too long because time was important. We thanked him and left.

The message was clear, Najja was at risk of having a stroke and we had to make a decision as to when she would have the surgery; therefore, within a week I called Dr. G and told him we wanted to go ahead with the surgery. He said he would check his schedule for an immediate date and get back to us.

In the meantime, we were advised to speak to Najja's hematologist about transfusion and the pre-operational procedures that needed to be done. He also said that Najja would have to take an angiogram, which would give a clear image of the stenosis and the Moyamoya Disease. We agreed to act on his suggestions immediately.

Over the next couple of days, we met with Dr. Sadanandan. She explained that a series of blood tests had to be done within a month of the procedure. She said that she would provide us with more information about the transfusion process so that we would clearly understand what was about to happen. I asked her where would the blood for the transfusion come from. She said that the hospital had blood reserved which was treated and stored for patients who needed it.

While taking care of things with Dr. Sadanandan, I took the opportunity to call the parent whose child had received brain surgery to treat the Moyamoya Disease. She answered the phone and I introduced myself, explaining the reason for my call. She stated that Dr. G. had saved her son's life. Additionally she said Dr. G was very professional, knowledgeable and compassionate. She talked about the history of her son's disease. She stated he complained of headaches and numbness in his arm but she did not think it was very serious. A year passed with nothing being done but one day her son had a seizure while at school. He was taken to the hospital and a series of tests performed yet the doctors were not sure why he had the seizure. After he was released she searched for a neurosurgeon. She found Dr. G and after reviewing her son's MRA and other test results he diagnosed him with Moyamoya Disease. Like many other people, she was not familiar with this illness and was perplexed about what to do. Her son had the disease on both sides of his brain, therefore, he had to have two surgeries within nine months to correct the disease. She explained that her son was doing well and she attributed this to Dr. G. She encouraged me not to worry and explained that Dr. G was capable, and would not recommend anyone else. I felt relieved and reassured by her words.

By then, it was October 2007 and there were lots of appointments to schedule. Najja had to get her yearly tests; Transcranial Doppler, cardiology exam, eye exam and abdominal sonogram. Since she was going to do an angiogram, there was no reason to do the MRA/MRI tests. The angiogram would give a clearer picture of what was going on in her brain. Before the angiogram was taken, she would have to be transfused. For me this was big because it would be her first transfusion and therefore we would have to prepare her for it. The transfusion was scheduled for December 5, 2007 and the angiogram was scheduled for December 7th.

The day of the transfusion came and I explained to Najja why she had to be transfused. She was not too concerned as she had seen quite a few children getting transfused in the past and it seemed like no big deal.

When we arrived to the hospital, we went straight to Dr. Sadanandan's office and the nurse took Najja to the examination room. From there an IV line was placed in her arm and blood was drawn to obtain her baseline blood count as well as to test the function of her liver before the transfusion.

After all the necessary procedures were done, Najja was placed in the day room where the transfusion would take place. She sat in a big burgundy convertible chair. Dr. Sadanandan and the nurse brought the bag with the transfused blood into the room and prepared to administer it to her. Before they started the transfusion, the nurse had to make sure that the right blood was being given to her, so she matched up the information printed on the bag to the information printed on Najja's arm band. After the information was confirmed, the nurse explained to Najja that once the procedure began, she should let her know if she felt dizzy, itchy, or had any tightness in her throat. Najja nodded in acknowledgement. It was at that point that the nurse started the transfusion.

I watched nervously as the process began. It was very simple, in that it was done the same way an IV had been done. Dr. Sadanandan and the nurse watched carefully for any allergic reactions from Najja. After about ten minutes both the nurse and Dr. Sadanandan seemed assured that Najja would be fine. On the other hand I remained nervous two and half hours, the length of the transfusion. When it was over, they disconnected her from the equipment and made her rest for an hour.

While we waited, I wanted to know what to expect now that she had been transfused. The doctor explained that the transfusion would cause her body to be like that of some-one who only had the Sickle Cell Trait. In some ways, I was relieved to know that she would be asymptomatic (without symptoms) for a few weeks.

On December 7, 2007 I drove Najja to the hospital to have the brain angiogram completed; it was done with-in an hour. Afterwards I scheduled an appointment for December 18, 2007 for her to see Dr. G. The meeting with Dr. G confirmed what we already knew about the stenosis on Najja's brain and the Moyamoya Disease. He suggested we have the surgery done on February 13, 2008 and we agreed.

In January 2008 I scheduled several appointments for Najja; with the cardiologist, pediatrician and hematolo-gist. The earliest available appointment for the cardiolo-gist was February 7th which was the day before her second transfusion and pre-operative exam and blood work. As a condition of the surgery, the patient should also see the hematologist located at the hospital where the surgery was to be performed.

Anxiety and fear crept in for both Najja and myself as the date for the surgery grew closer. There were all types of thoughts going through my mind, mostly that she would not survive the procedure. From one negative thought to another I became overwhelmed; she would have a negative reaction to the anesthesia, she would stop breathing, she would have a stroke, the thoughts continued. A few days before the surgery, Najja admitted her fear and cried. She asked, "Why did everything bad happen to me?" Lovingly with comfort and reassurance, I told her that this was not bad; but sometimes things happen and we have to fix them. Taking her hand, I prayed and asked God to see her through and to release her from all of her fears while giving her strength and courage. Additionally I told her that everyone was praying for including our pastor and prayer team from the church.

The day before the surgery, February 12th, Najja was admitted to the hospital. The surgery was scheduled for early the next morning. I packed all the things she needed; her nightgown, slippers, panties, robe, washcloth and toiletries. That night I checked her into the hospital and settled her in. I spent the night with her because only one parent was allowed to stay with her.

February 13th, the day of the surgery, Dr. G, the anesthesiologist and another doctor came to see Najja. They reviewed her chart and did a basic physical examination before telling her they would see her in the operating area. Half an hour passed before the nursing assistant came to take her to the waiting area for the surgery. By then, her dad had arrived along with my mother.

Once in the waiting area, the doctors came back. It was count down time, they were ready to do the procedure. My baby was about to have brain surgery, how scary was that! As she was wheeled into the operating room, I followed behind. My heart raced, my palms sweated, there was a knot in my throat and I tried to fight my tears. I held her hand and lowered my head to kiss her forehead. As I kissed her, she said, "Mommy, I don't want you to leave, can you stay with me?" I whispered in her ear telling her I love her and I wished I could stay, but I was not allowed to do so. I told her that I would be waiting for her right outside the door and I would see her once the surgery was over. I told her the doctors promised to take the very best care of her. Just then, the anesthesiologist told me it was time to give her the anesthesia. She said I could stay with her as the anesthesia was given and she drifted off to sleep. I was numb, my eyes swelled up with tears, my heart ached and my nerves were shattered. It was unreal! With tears streaming heavily down my face I turned around and walked out of the operating room.

Her dad met me in the hallway and he tried to console me as we walked slowly to the waiting room. There we sat for three and a half hours waiting patiently for the surgery to end. Her dad did not say much but I could tell he was also in distress. He folded his arms and stared blankly at the ceiling. That was the longest three hours we have ever had to endure. It really is hard to explain how heartwrenching it was for me; for us to see our little girl go through such a big procedure. The experience was very frightening.

Finally the surgery was over; with my head resting on my husband's lap I looked toward the operating room and saw the anesthesiologist walking toward us. Keeping my eyes on her face I wanted to gauge her expression – whether happy, disappointed or sad. I waited anxiously for her. She said, "Your little girl is a trooper, she did well. Are you ready to see her?" My husband and I looked at each other, hugged then rushed to the recovery room to be with her. Since only one of us could visit her at a time, I went first. The doctor advised me to put on a sterilized gown, pants and shoes and allowed me to walk to her bed. She was still under the effects of anesthesia and it took her a while to regain total consciousness. I wanted to scream, "MY BABY SURVIVED EDAS SURGERY!"

The first thing she said when she opened her eyes was "Mommy, I am okay and I have a new brain." "Yes baby, you are okay!" I responded. She spent two additional hours in the recovery room just for observation. Her next stop was the ICU (Intensive Care Unit). She spent a day or two there so that her progress could be monitored. The atmosphere in the unit was very intense, with doctors and nurses everywhere watching and charting patients intently.

Najja was placed in a big room by herself. It had lots of space for family members to visit. It felt comfortable. Within an hour of us being there, the doctors came in to check on her and to explain the reason for her being there. "It is important for her to be monitored closely within the next 24 hours," they said. They explained that even though she seemed to be doing exceptionally well, she was still not out of the woods and things could change. "What things?" I asked. Well, she was still at risk of hemorrhaging, she could have a stroke, or she could go into crisis so it was very important that she rested.

After spending two days in the ICU, she was moved to the regular pediatric floor. Once on that floor the supervision lessened and she was able to eat, move around, interact with the other patients and have additional visitors. Her stay in that unit was also very short. She only spent two days there before we were told she could go home. As we prepared to leave we were told the necessary precautions to follow. She was given instructions to take it easy and rest. Antibiotics were prescribed to fight any infections as well as pain medicine. We were also given instructions on how to care for the wound.

The day Najja came home I was happy on more than one level. The surgery had gone well and she had no foreseeable complications. The possibility of Najja having a stroke had decreased so I was especially excited. As she healed, new arteries would grow eventually enabling her to receive more oxygen and blood flow to her brain. What a relief!

Within two weeks of the EDAS procedure, Najja had an appointment to see Dr. G. so he could examine the wound and take out some of the stitches. He advised us that she would be able to return to school two weeks after the appointment with him. Najja was so excited about that because she wanted to go back to school and reconnect with her friends. I found her eagerness to return to some normalcy amazing. She was full of life and a lot of energy.

Another four months passed before she returned to Dr. G's office which was then July 2008. The purpose for this visit was to see if the regeneration of the new arteries had begun. Prior to the visit, I had to take Najja to do a post-operational MRA. The MRA would show the progression of the new blood vessels.

The day of the appointment came and both her father and I took her to the appointment. We were anxious to hear what Dr. G had to say about the effectiveness of the surgery. As he began to examine her he pressed two of his fingers against her temporal lobe. The purpose of doing this was to check her pulse. If she had one, this would mean the arteries were beginning to grow. Over time the pulse should increase in strength. Next he looked at the MRA to view the arteries and explained that she would grow enough new arteries which would allow her to get sufficient blood flow and oxygen. I asked him what would happen if new arteries did not grow and he said, "nothing, we would return to the original course of treatment or discuss another course of action with her hematologist."

I asked him how long it would be before Najja's brain would heal completely. "One year," he said. I also wanted to know if the Moyamoya Disease could return. "Yes, it could in a separate area of the brain," he replied. I also asked him if Najja had the stenosis on the left side of the brain. He said, "no." Additionally I asked him what would happen to the area where she has the stenosis. He explained that the area would stay the same because the stenosis cannot be fixed.

Dr. G continued to explain that Najja should continue to do well and would not have to see him for the next six to seven months. He cautioned that if she developed any headaches, dizziness or eye pain, we should not hesitate to call him. He also told us after her year healing period, she should be able to start preparing for the transplant. That was great news for all of us. We thanked Dr. G for helping Najja and then we left.

From July 2008 to January 2009, Najja did exceptionally well. She had no Sickle Cell related illnesses, no headaches, eye pain or any other sickness. However on February 2, 2009, she woke up and came into my room and laid on my bed. She complained of a pain in her left eye. I asked her how intense was the pain and she said it was mild. I grabbed the Motrin and gave some to her. Within a few minutes she threw up. I went into the kitchen and boiled some ginger and made her a cup tea. It took 30 minutes for the eye pain and stomach discomfort to go away.

On February 8, 2009, we had an appointment to see Dr. G. At that time it had been one year since Najja had the EDAS surgery and she had done exceptionally well. Once we arrived to his office, it did not take long for him to examine her. He explained that by then she should have regenerated enough new arteries in order to supply her brain with sufficient oxygen and blood flow. I told him that she had one episode of eye pain in January, however it was mild. He replied that I should monitor any further episodes and if they became constant over time, I should make an appointment to see him.

On February 9th, we had an appointment to meet with Dr. Del Toro. He requested a meeting because he wanted to sit with both Najja and Justin in order to discuss the transplant procedure with them specifically. He wanted to make sure that they were both on board with the procedure and that they were not doing it because they felt they had no choice. Dr. Del Toro told them that he had a deep concern for Najja and her feelings because she would be directly affected by the procedure. He went on to tell them that he wanted them to ask any questions they had. It was Justin who took the opportunity to ask the first question. He wanted to know how the transplant would help Najja. Dr. Del Toro responded by letting him know that was a good question. He continued to explain that the Bone Marrow Transplant would help Najja be cured of Sickle Cell. He continued to explain that presently, Najja's bone marrow makes defective red blood cells which make her sick sometimes. "However, by destroying it with chemotherpay and replacing it with yours, she will have a new bone marrow that makes healthy red blood cells." Dr. Del Toro continued by saying once she received the bone marrow, it would take about four to six weeks before new cells would begin growing or engrafting. Najja wanted to know if the procedure would hurt. Dr. Del Toro told her no. He said, however, the chemotherpay could cause many different kinds of discomfort; like mouth sores, skin rashes, diarrhea, nausea, vomiting, tiredness and hair loss. He also pointed out in addition the chemotherpay could also cause itching, high blood pressure, dizziness and seizures. These were just a few of the side effects she could experience. Najja then asked how long would it take for her hair to fall out and whether it would fall out all at once. Dr. Del Toro responded that it would take about two to three weeks into the transplant before she would see any sign of hair loss. He explained that her hair would fall out in patches. He also told her that besides hair loss, her finger and toe nails would turn dark, her skin would get darker and would get really dry. Najja asked if her family would be able to visit her. Dr. Del Toro responded that once the transplant had begun, only mom and dad would be able to visit and stay with her at night. He said that was because her white blood cell count would be very low and she would be at a high risk of getting infections, the less visitors she had would be the better.

Najja persisted with her questions. She wanted to know whether she would feel sick from the chemotherapy. Dr. Del Toro told her yes, the chemotherapy would make her feel very tired and her energy level would be very low. He told her that she would be sleeping a lot. He said that at times she would experience a range of emotions, such as sadness, fear, anger and sometimes happiness. Najja then asked if she would be able to eat. Dr. Del Toro assured her that she would be able to eat. He said, however that she would not want to because the chemotherapy would take away her appetite and the mouth sores would make it difficult to chew and swallow her food. He continued by saying that from his experience, most kids eat very little during the procedure. They preferred to drink beverages such as ginger ale, juice or water. When they did eat it was mostly items such as noodles, macaroni, applesauce, jello and soups. He also added that she would lose a lot of weight. He said if he saw that she lost more than fifteen pounds and could not eat solid foods, then she would be fed by a tube that would be placed in her stomach. He told her not to worry about that because it rarely happens. At that point, I wanted to know if she had to get radiation. He said no, as it was not required for her procedure. I also wanted to know what would sustain her once the chemotherapies wiped out her bone marrow. He responded by explaining that blood transfusions, platelet transfusions and many other medications would remedy that situation. I told him that I was told that the chemotherapy caused infertility, and if so what could we do to prevent that? He responded by saying that the medications would certainly make her sterile however, we could have tissue removed from her ovaries and freeze it until she was ready to have children. He said that the procedure is called ovarian harvesting. He also mentioned that it was a fairly simple procedure and that he knew an expert in that field. He said the only thing was that we would have to travel to Westchester to get the procedure done and also that it would cost us about $15,000 because insurance did not cover the procedure. He then gave us the doctor's name and phone number so that we could make an appointment to meet with him.

Next Justin wanted to know how the marrow would be taken from him and would he be awake through the procedure. Dr. Del Toro explained to Justin that on the day that the actual transplant would take place, he would be admitted to the hospital. He would be taken to the operating room and put to sleep. Once he was asleep the doctors would use several long needles to pull the marrow from both sides of his hips. Dr. Del Toro explained that the procedure would take about two hours. Once the procedure was done, he would go to the recovery room for a few hours and then go to the pediatric floor for another day. At the end of that day, he would go home. He also wanted to know whether the procedure hurt. Dr. Del Toro told him that the procedure would not hurt while it was being done because he would be asleep. However, he would feel moderate aches and pain; something like the pain felt after a bad fall. He told Justin that he would have to stay home from school for a few days so that he could recuperate sufficiently.

Najja then wanted to know what should she do while she was receiving the bone marrow. Dr. Del Toro told her that would be entirely up to her. He told her that she could sleep, she could lie down or she could sit up and watch the procedure. He added that she could play her DS, or she could talk to her mom or her dad. Najja also asked if she could die while she was getting the bone marrow. Dr. Del Toro looked at both Najja and Justin and honestly answered "yes." He continued to explain that with all procedures people could die but he believed that would not happen because she was strong and was in good health. At that point both children began to cry and the room became silent for a few moments. Breaking the silence, I asked if arrangements could be made for us to see the transplant unit. Dr. Del Toro said that was definitely possible, however, he would have to call the unit and make arrangements for us to see it.

Then he recommended that we begin to think about a date for the transplant. We told him we would definitely want Najja to finish the school year. I further added that we had already planned our summer vacation, therefore we could begin to think about dates in September or October.

On March 24th, the children and I had a meeting with the child life specialist of the transplant unit. Her job was mainly to make sure that all of Najja's social, emotional and psychological needs were met once she was admitted to the transplant unit and the procedure had begun. She said that she would be the one responsible for planning the daily schedule of different activities such as a time for school, games, as well as having time with Najja to talk about her feelings and concerns. She said that the purpose for this meeting was to get to know them better. She pointed out that she had a lot of questions for Najja and Justin and she hoped they had a lot of questions for her. She began her questioning by asking them about the things they liked to do; such as their favorite sports, favorite music, and places they liked to go. She asked whether they played any instruments and if yes, what were they. Najja told her that she played the guitar and Justin told her he played the piano and the saxophone.

She talked about her function as a Child Life Specialist. She said it was a very special job because she had the opportunity to meet so many children who really needed her help in coping with their illnesses and being in the hospital. She said she felt fulfilled in helping them while they went through the transplants. The meeting lasted about an hour and the children left feeling very relieved because many of their questions were answered.

It should be noted that from February to the beginning of May, Najja had done fairly well. She did not experience any sickle related episode. However, May 9th to the 11th, she had a fever and a sore throat. I called Dr. Sadanandan on the 11th and told her what was happening. She said it sounded as if Najja had a virus and it would take a few days to go away. She advised me to give her Motrin and to monitor the temperature to see that it did not go past 102. After a few days, the fever and sore throat were gone and Najja began to feel better.

From May 29th to June 6th, we were in St. Martin/ St. Marteen for Najja's 13th birthday. While we were there she had no episodes. However, when we returned home, I

noticed that she had a slight limp. I told her father to observe her walk. He did and thought there was nothing
unusual about her. However, I thought her stride was different and she was definitely limping. I waited about a week
to see if the limp went away; it did not so I asked Najja if
she had fallen and injured her leg. She said no. I also asked
her if her leg hurt or was it bothering her in any way. She
responded no.

A few weeks passed and she was still limping so I made
an appointment for August 4th for her to see Dr. Sawicki,
the pediatrician. On the day of the appointment, Dr. Sawicki
examined Najja thoroughly and concluded that the limp was
very slight. She added that she didn't think anything drastic had happened and over time the limp should disappear.
I went home feeling dissatisfied, so the next day, I called
Dr. Sadanandan and explained to her that Najja had been
limping since the first week in June. I added that I had taken
her to see Dr. Sawicki the day prior and after doing a comprehensive examination on Najja, Dr. Sawicki did not think
anything unusual had happened to her leg. Dr. Sadanandan
suggested I make an appointment to bring Najja in so that
she could examine her because based on Najja's history with
the stenosis, something neurological might have happened
to her leg. She suggested I bring Najja into her office on
August 12th.

On the day of the appointment, as Najja walked into the
office, Dr. Sadanandan recognized from the way she walked
that she had experienced a neurological disturbance. Therefore she took her into one of the rooms to examine her leg
further. When she was done, she noted that she definitely
thought that Najja had suffered a mini stroke. However
in order for her to confirm the findings, she said an MRA
with contrast and an MRI should be done immediately.

She called the Radiology Department and scheduled an appointment for August 19th. She said that once the test results came back, she would call me. She added that in the meantime, I should schedule an appointment to see Dr. S, the neurologist because she would be the best person to examine Najja and to discuss the findings of the MRA and the MRI. Before, we left Dr. Sadanandan's office, I asked her to send a copy of the report to Dr. Sawicki, Dr. G and Dr. Del Toro. I also asked for a copy for my records.

On August 26th, I took Najja to see Dr. S. She observed Najja as she walked into her office. She asked her to sit on the examining table so that she could examine her leg. Dr. S tapped Najja's knees to test her reflexes. She then asked Najja to wiggle and flex her toes. Dr. S continued the examination by asking Najja to walk on her heel, then on her toes. Najja then had to balance on her right leg then the left. She then asked Najja to do a series of leg motions to get an idea of the extent of the damage. Dr. S read the MRA report and said that it did not indicate that Najja had any new strokes only the same old ischemias (mini strokes) that she had in the past. However she said that she thought Najja had a small occurrence in the area of the brain that controlled the motion in her leg and that was why she had the slight limp. She continued to explain that even though Najja had the EDAS procedure to improve blood flow, the Sickle Cell Disease continued to interfere with the arteries. The only solution at that point was to get the Bone Marrow Transplant done as quickly as possible in order to get rid of the disease. She also suggested that in the meantime, Najja should start physical therapy. I asked her to send her findings to each doctor. I made a special request for her to make sure Dr. Del Toro received a copy of her findings immediately.

The next day, I called Dr. Del Toro to discuss the meeting I had with Dr. S. I explained to him all that transpired during the meeting and I also told him that he should receive a report from Dr. S in a matter of days. He advised me that we should set a date for the Bone Marrow Transplant. He checked his planner and suggested October 19th. I told him that date was acceptable to me however, I would have to let my husband, Najja and Justin know. He also said that he would have his assistant call me to begin to set up the appointments that were necessary before the transplant would start. He remarked that both children would have to do a series of blood work and physical examinations about 30 days before the procedure. He noted that Najja especially, would need to see an ophthalmologist, a cardiologist, a dentist, a pulmonologist, a pediatrician, and the hematologist. She would also need a chest x-ray and a pulmonary function test done. We would also have to meet with the doctor who would possibly do the ovarian harvesting procedure.

The month of September was very busy for us. There were many different appointments to be kept as well as a transfusion and the ovarian harvesting procedure to be done. I called the ovarian harvesting doctor and he agreed to meet with us September 24th. On the day of the appointment, he told us that the procedure is performed by placing a small incision adjacent to Najja's hip bones. He said that he would use a small instrument to insert through the incisions to remove the tissue from her ovaries. He explained that the procedure was an outpatient procedure taking about 90 minutes. Najja would go to a recovery room for observation and would be able to go home if her vital signs remained normal.

On Friday, October 16th, I took Najja into the hospital to get transfused because the transplant would start on

October 19th, the following Monday. As the transfusion began, Dr. Del Toro's partner, Dr. R filled in for him that day; she came into the room and said she needed to speak to me and I should step outside the room. She appeared to be somewhat dismayed. As she spoke, she had the most mind boggling news. According to her, one of the blood tests that Najja had taken came back positive for Hepatitis C virus. As first, I was not sure what she was talking about because I did not know what Hepatitis C was. Dr. R continued to explain that Hepatitis C is an infection that is caused by a virus that attacks the liver. It is contracted by being in contact with an infected person's blood. She explained that people get the disease by sharing drug needles with an infected person, using an infected person's razor or toothbrush or having sexual intercourse with an infected person. Dr. R added that the disease can be contracted through blood transfusion. I listened carefully, but I was bewildered and furious. The conversation sounded unreal. I interrupted her and told her somewhere along the line, someone made a mistake, this could not be true. At this point my eyes were filled with tears and I was at a loss for words.

I managed to ask Dr. R where on earth Najja contracted such a virus, since she was not a drug user, she was not sexually active and she had only had three transfusions; all of which were done at her hematologist's office. I had to take several deep breaths because I wanted to scream. I asked her what would be the next course of action. She responded by saying that she would have Najja redo the blood work however, we would have to wait for a week for the results to come back. I shook my head in disbelief and asked her how should I explain that to Najja. She responded by saying that was the difficult part and she thought it would be best not to go into a lot of details with her until the test results were confirmed. Dr. R felt that the best thing to tell Najja was that the transplant had to be postponed because one of the blood tests had to be redone because the result seemed to be incorrect.

The following Monday, I took Najja back to the hospital to retake the blood test. Within a week I received a phone call from Dr. R who told me that the result was back and it was negative, Najja did not have Hepatitis C. That was great news for us. She suggested we set a new transplant date for November 23rd. I told her I would discuss it with my husband and the children then get back to her and Dr. Del Toro.

After speaking to my husband, Najja and Justin, we all agreed that November 23rd would be the date to begin the Bone Marrow Transplant. I contacted Dr. Del Toro to let him know that we were in agreement with the date. He informed me that he would have his secretary reschedule Najja and Justin to redo some of the blood work that was previously done because the results had to be within 30 days prior to the procedure.

Over the next few weeks, I took Najja and Justin to redo all the necessary blood work and to see the remaining specialists; Najja was examined to get an idea of her baseline health. Justin also had to see the pediatrician and the hematologist to check his baseline health. When all the appointments were taken care of, Najja was ready to start the pre-conditioning for the Bone Marrow Transplant and Justin was ready to be her donor.

The Transplant

❦

As a parent, from my perspective a Bone Marrow Transplant is an intense and risky procedure which seemed unimaginable. It was difficult for me to watch my child go through such a complicated process, not knowing what the outcome would be. It took every bit of inner strength to watch her go through this transplant. My physical endurance was mandatory because the days were long; I stayed with her throughout the days; monitored her progress, fed her when she was hungry, cleaned her when the nurses were too busy, made sure she took her medications, and comforted her when the moments were daunting. The days were long but the nights were even longer; it was difficult to sleep in a hospital with the staff constantly coming in and out of the rooms; additionally, I felt a need to keep my eyes on her continually. Mentally and emotionally I had to remain courageous and optimistic for her sake believing she would come through the process with minimal complication. Throughout the process I remained prayerful, making sure my feelings were under control.

Najja, on the other hand, was a champ throughout most of the procedure. Mentally she was like a solid structure weathering a furious storm. Emotionally, she remained steadfast. She rarely shed a tear or complained. Her emotions remained intact and her spirit was amazing.

The procedure began on November 23, 2009; she was admitted to the hospital to undergo a surgical procedure which involved placing a central venous catheter near her heart. This was a tube-like instrument that would allow her to get chemotherapy into her central vein and to have blood drawn and medication given without her having to be injected with needles repeatedly. The procedure took about two hours. Then she was transferred to the Bone Marrow Transplant Unit where she remained throughout the transplant and until she was well enough to go home.

Throughout that first day, Dr. Del Toro came into Najja's room several times to check on her. He explained to us that before the night was over, she would have an exchange transfusion. The purpose for the exchange transfusion was to lower the amount of sickle hemoglobin to prevent her from going into crisis while she received the chemo the next day. He also stated in addition to the exchange transfusion, she would begin to receive some of the necessary medications like morphine for pain, Benadryl to prevent any allergic reaction and Fosphenytoin to prevent seizures. He said that the latter medication would have to be taken for six months after the transplant. He explained to Najja the reason she had to take the medications and told her he felt she was doing great.

Dr. Del Toro suggested that Najja rest as the following day (Tuesday, November 24) would be a big day because the pre-transplant conditioning would begin before the actual transplant would start. We followed Dr. Del Toro's advice for Najja to get some rest.

At 8:00 a.m. Najja was awakened by two of the unit nurses. They were ready to administer the first dosage of chemo. It was called Busulfan which was given to completely destroy her bone marrow so that her body could accept her brother's bone marrow. It was administered for duration of four days (from the Tuesday to Saturday). Then she had one day of rest before starting another chemo therapy regime.

As the nurses came in, I felt nervous. I did not let Najja know how I felt. I just held her hand and asked her if she was ready to start. She nodded her head to indicate yes. One of the nurses turned to her and encouraged her not to worry because most of the children usually did not have any reaction to the chemo. Nevertheless, throughout the first phase of the treatment, I watched her carefully. She had no significant reaction. She only vomited once and remained in good spirits.

The next day (Wednesday, November 25) Najja continued to do well. She was up talking and playing with her Grandmother Daphne. She also ate most of her meals that day. By late afternoon, however, she threw up again. The nurses watched her carefully for any other reactions. They reminded us that vomiting was a common side-effect from the chemo. Dr. Del Toro also came in and examined Najja and according to him, she was doing well. He called her a trooper with an amazing spirit.

The following day, November 26th was Thanksgiving Day and Najja remained in good spirits. Her father and I tried to make the day as normal for her as we could. He brought in a well-prepared Thanksgiving meal for her, even though she did not eat much. We talked and played with her as much as she could withstand. She even had a few visitors; her two older sisters Tishanna and Aisha came to spend some time with her. They made it their duty to encourage her by praying and reminding her that God will see her through.

Later that same evening, Dr. Del Toro came in to examine Najja. He noticed that she seemed off balance as she stood up and began walking back and forth for him. He became very concerned because the chemo could cause her to have a seizure. He then called for the neurology team to come in to evaluate her. Within half an hour the members of the neurology team came and examined her. They noted that she did have a slight imbalance. It did not appear to be serious; however, they did recommend a MRA with contrast be done in order to make sure she was not having a neurological disturbance. After the team left, I asked Dr. Del Toro what could be expected next. He said that each patient responded differently to the chemotherapies and the procedure. As a result, she might continue the way she was, with little or no complications, or she could develop serious complications at any point. He then stated that we should take it one day at a time because she was doing well thus far.

Friday November 27th came and Najja continued to do fairly well. She had no vomiting or diarrhea, she only complained of tiredness and she did not eat much. She was scheduled to have the MRA later that evening. Throughout the day, she basically rested until it was time for her to go for the test.

On Saturday morning, November 28th, at 8:00 a.m. Najja started two new chemotherapy regimens – Cyclo-phosphamide and Rabbit Anti-Thmocyte Globulin (ATG). The purpose of these regimens was to keep her immune system suppressed so that the new marrow would not be rejected.

At first she did not have an immediate reaction to the chemos, however, by late Saturday evening she had a fever, severe chills, vomiting and diarrhea. She was very weak and tired. That was one of her worst moments since the transplant started. She had a very difficult time throughout the night and there was little sleep for either of us. All I could do was sit by her bedside and rub her back and legs and watch, wait and hope that she pulled through without getting worse. That stage of the transplant was difficult and scary. I tried really hard to keep my emotions intact but I could not hold back my tears or manage my anxiety.

Over the next few days, she slept a lot, did not eat much and vomited continuously. In addition, she had frequent diarrhea and stomach aches. As a result of sickness, she was weak and could not move her body, open her eyes; she could barely talk to anyone.

In addition to the vomiting, diarrhea, and stomach aches, she also developed another fever along with sneezing, running nose and her eyes were blood shot red. So, I asked the nurses to call Dr. Del Toro so that he could examine Najja. Upon seeing her, Dr. Del Toro became concerned because the symptoms she displayed could become life threatening if she was not treated immediately. He was very concerned about the fever because that was an indication that she might have an infection of some kind; the problem with getting an infection at that stage of the transplant was that her immune system was very compromised and her body had very little defense in fighting off any kind of infections. Dr. Del Toro prescribed Tama flu as a precaution against the flu. In addition he had her blood drawn and sent to the lab to test for specific viral infections.

Within a few hours most of the results came back from the lab indicating that she had no signs of infection. Therefore Dr. Del Toro concluded that the symptoms Najja had might have been a reaction to the chemotherapy medications. By December 1st, the fever was gone, but the runny nose, the blood shot eyes, the tiredness and weakness continued. She still did not eat or drink much either. However, the good thing was this was the last day she would receive the chemotherapies. It was also the day she would get a plasma exchange. This procedure was necessary to decrease her antibodies so when she received the new bone marrow, her body would not reject it.

By late evening, once the chemotherapy had stopped, she felt better. We could tell because, for the first time in days, she sat up and asked if she could watch TV. She was also hungry and she even had a little smile on her face. The following day, December 2nd was a rest day for Najja as there was no chemo. Her spirit had lifted. She ate, talked with her grandmother and watched TV most of the day. Physically, she felt less tired and weak, but she still had a runny nose which Dr. Del Toro and the nurses were still very concerned about. As a result, they kept a close eye on her throughout that day.

As Najja went through the pre-conditioning for the Bone Marrow Transplant, Justin was at home preparing for his admission to the hospital the following morning, December 3rd so that he could give the bone marrow. That was a big day for both of them. Najja would receive a life altering procedure and her brother, Justin, would be the one to change her life forever; a life without Sickle Cell Disease. What a blessing!

The following morning, Justin was admitted to the hospital and taken to the operating room where he was placed under anesthesia. Dr. Del Toro and his team began the process of taking the bone marrow from him. Once he was asleep the doctors turned him on his stomach. They then used several large needles to pull the marrow from each side of his posterior Iliac crest (the lower part of his back, near his hip bone). While the procedure was being performed on Justin, Najja was in her room waiting to hear from us in regards to Justin's progress. The procedure was painless, but it took about three hours, from beginning to end. Once the procedure was finished, he was taken to the recovery room for a few hours. He was later transferred to the pediatric unit for another day of observation before he was released.

December 3rd was a big day. It was transplant infusion day. The doctors called it Day 0 because it was considered to be the starting point of Najja's new life – a life without Sickle Cell Disease. She was very excited and upbeat. She talked and played with her Child Life Specialist. She watched TV and ate small amounts of food. By late evening, Dr. Del Toro and his team came into her room to do a final physical exam before the transplant would begin. They also informed us that the infusion would take place about 8:00 p.m. We were filled with mixed emotions of excitement and fear at the same time. We felt afraid because we were not sure how her body would react once she was infused but we were excited because she was about to have a new lease on life, one without Sickle Cell Disease; no crisis, no eye pain and the stenosis would be less likely to progress. She would have a life free of pain and suffering. This would be awesome for her.

As Dr. Del Toro examined Najja, he informed us of the various things that could happen. One thing was that Najja's blood pressure could get very high which could cause her to have a seizure or a stroke; especially because of the underlying vascular issues she had previously. He also said that her kidneys and the liver could be affected, and that she could have respiratory failure. However, he assured us that there was preventative measure in place to combat most issues that may arise.

It was then early evening – 4:30 pm to be exact and Dr. Del Toro spent most of the day preparing the bone marrow, evaluating Najja, reviewing her files and making sure that everything was in place for the procedure. He told us that things were going according to plan and Najja seemed to be doing great. We simply had to wait for the appointed time. By 8:00 pm the unit nurse informed us that Dr. Del Toro was on his way to the unit to begin the procedure. Once again the nurses took Najja's blood pressure, checked temperature, and tested her oxygen level to get a baseline. Then the unit door opened and Dr. Del Toro came in along with another nurse carrying the bone marrow. Dr. Del Toro signaled to Najja and asked her if she was ready. She gave him her usual thumbs up and he responded by telling her "Let's do this." She smiled. The nurse proceeded to hang the bag with the bone marrow on the IV pole, which also had another 10 bags of medications. He connected the tube to her central line and within minutes the infusion began. The bone marrow cells made their way through her blood stream and began to settle into the place where the original cells were located.

As the infusion took place, Dr. Del Toro sat on the edge of the chair behind the nurses' station. His fingers were interlocked under his chin as he watched Najja intently to see how her body would respond. For a while the procedure was going along perfectly, but midway, her blood pressure started to elevate. At first, Dr. Del Toro just observed the elevation, however the numbers kept increasing. As her pressure reached 145/90 he instructed the nurse to give blood pressure medication to decrease her pressure. He also instructed Najja to urinate immediately because the medication would build up fluid in the body which could affect the kidneys. From that moment on, Dr. Del Toro and the nurse kept a keen eye on Najja, monitoring her pressure and her other vital signs. Other than the increased pressure, the procedure had gone well and within an hour the infusion had ended.

The day after the infusion, (December 4th) Najja did not feel well; she complained that her stomach was upset and she vomited about four times. She continued to have diarrhea and did not eat much food. Additionally, her blood pressure remained high. As a result, she was given blood pressure medication once again to keep it under control.

Dr. Del Toro explained that it would take time for her body to heal and readjust itself; therefore, it would take time for the vomiting, diarrhea and stomach pains to lessen. He also added that as time moved forward, she would feel a little less tired and her appetite would increase slowly. Additionally, she would be watched carefully for the many complications that could occur after a transplant; especially grafting of the bone marrow.

According to him, the process would take anywhere from four to six weeks. In the meantime, blood was drawn every day to check her white counts, platelets and her hemoglobin to monitor the levels. In addition, the levels for her liver, kidney functions, iron, magnesium and potassium were also checked. She continued to receive the necessary medications; Cyclosporine and Methotrexate to prevent Graft vs. Host Disease. The latter two medications were given on days 1, 3, 6 and 11 after transplant. She continued to receive Dilantin to prevent seizures, Actigal to protect her liver, Mycelex to protect her mouth and throat from infections, Zofran for nausea, and Benadryl to prevent her from having any allergic reaction from any of the medications. In addition, she was given a few blood transfusions when her hemoglobin dropped below the required margin.

The next day, December 5th, Najja continued to feel weak and tired. She complained that her stomach was still upset and as a result, she ate no food and she slept most of that day. The following day, Sunday, December 6th, Najja woke up feeling better. This was apparent because the first thing she did after waking up was ask for something to eat. She wanted her breakfast so she ate hash browns, fruit and a cup of ginger tea. Throughout the day, she ate fairly well and did not vomit at all.

Throughout the remaining days of the transplant Najja continued to get better day-after-day. By December 17th, which was 14 days after infusion, the bone marrow started to show signs of growth. Her white counts were 200 which was a good sign. The nurses were excited because once growth had began, it would rapidly and steadily increase until it reached the point where it would be safe for her to leave her special room and eventually go home. By December 22nd, Najja's white counts were 9,000 and as a result,

Dr. Del Toro assured us that she would definitely be home by New Year's Day. On December 26th, we got the word that she would be discharged on December 28th. That was more good news for Najja. She was so excited. I was overjoyed, as she had made it through this difficult journey and had done so well.

The day of her discharge came and the whole process took most of the day because the nurses had to sit with me to make sure I understood the importance of her home care. This included my home being cleaned thoroughly and free from dust, plants and pets. The carpet had to be taken up or cleaned properly. The food she ate had to be fully cooked. She could only have fruits that were peeled, such as oranges, bananas, grapefruits, pears, peaches and apples. The only people she could be exposed to were the ones who lived in our house, absolutely no visitors. The only time she could go outdoors was if she were going to the clinic and at such time she would have to wear a mask over her nose to prevent her from contracting any kind of viral or bacterial infections.

The nurses also reiterated that Najja's weekly visits to the clinic were vitally important. She was scheduled to be in the clinic three times a week: Mondays, Wednesday and Fridays for the first three months. Depending on how well she was doing, it would be reduced to once or twice a week for the second trimester. They added that another important part of Najja's recovery was making sure that she took all her medications and took them on time. She was prescribed eleven different medications. These medications ranged from Neupogen, which she took every other day to help increase her white cells, to Cytosporine which was taken three times a day to help to suppress her immune system. She had to take Dilantin three times a day to prevent seizures as a result of taking the Cytosporine. She also had to take Valacyclovir, once a day to help to protect her from viral infections, Fluconazole once a day to prevent fungal infections, Penicillin twice a day to prevent bacterial infections, Clotrimazole to prevent thrush in her mouth and Magnesium Oxide three times a day to keep her magnesium level from falling below level. The Cytosporine also decreased magnesium levels. She took Famotidine twice a day to protect her stomach, Zofran twice a day to prevent nausea and Actigall once a week to maintain her liver function and Lopressor to maintain her blood pressure.

Keeping track of the medications and the times she had to take them required a lot of focus and time management. Thus, the first three months of Najja's home care were difficult and long. The days seemed endless because we had to go the clinic three to four times a week and spent six to seven hours there. The nights were sleepless because I had to make sure she took her medications and many nights Najja would wake up because she just did not feel well.

On January 4, 2010, one week after Najja had come home from the hospital after the Bone Marrow Transplant, something new happened. She went to use the bathroom and had complained of pain as she urinated. Upon wiping herself, she had noticed that the tissue had a pink streak. I told her to wipe again and still there was a pink stain on the tissue. So throughout the day, I monitored her carefully in order to see whether the situation would worsen or improve. Najja continued to complain about the pain and the pink streak became more apparent, therefore, by late evening, I called Dr. Del Toro and told him what was happening. He said the pain and the pink streak could be the result of several things. He said that Najja could have a urinary tract infection, she could be starting to menstruate or that she was beginning to develop the BK virus. He said that the latter condition was one of the side effects from the chemo. However he did not want to go into details over the phone so he asked me to bring her into the hospital the first thing the next day.

Upon arriving at the hospital the following day, Najja was seen immediately. Her blood was drawn and a physical examination done. Dr. Del Toro spoke to her at length so that he could get a clear picture from Najja as to what she had seen and to find out how she felt. After his conversation with Najja, Dr. Del Toro asked me to step outside of the examining room so that we could speak privately. He explained that Najja seemed to have the early stage of the BK virus, but he could not be sure until the blood work and urine sample were done to confirm the virus presence. He said that if it was actually confirmed that she had the virus, it would be very dangerous as well as hard to treat. Thus in the event it was confirmed, it had to be treated immediately and aggressively or else it would worsen rapidly and could be fatal. He explained that BK stood for the initials of the person who had discovered the virus. He said that the BK Virus caused the bladder to bleed and that in order to treat it Najja would have to take a very strong antibiotic called Cidofovir. However, before taking it she would have to take another medication called Probenecid to protect her kidneys. This was because the Cidofovir had a devastating effect on the kidneys and could cause them to shut down. In addition to taking both medications, she had to have a lot of fluids via IV to flush the kidneys. This meant that she would get IV from home for as long as she was on the Cidofovir. He said that a nurse would come to our home to show me how to set up the IV line at night and then how to flush it in the morning. Dr. Del Toro also explained that in addition to the medication regimens and the IV fluids, the second part of the treatment that was absolutely necessary in treating the BK Virus was Hyperbaric Therapy. That was a treatment that would allow her to breathe in 100% oxygen from inside a pressurized Hyperbaric Chamber. That treatment would greatly increase the concentration of oxygen that would go to her organs and tissues in her body and thus stimulate growth of new blood vessels. He said that over time the new blood vessels would promote healing in the chronically-wounded areas. In Najja's case it would be her in bladder. He explained that that part of treatment would help with the healing process of her bladder.

Dr. Del Toro explained how the physical structure of the Hyperbaric Chamber was set up. He said that it actually looked like a submarine on the outside. On the inside there were about six to eight rows of seats on each side of the isle with oxygen masks hanging from the ceiling. The best visual he could give me of how the seats were arranged was that of the seating arrangements on an aircraft with the only difference being that of the patients facing each other while seated. He further explained that Najja would need 30 treatments, which would consist of 1½ hour per day for 30 days. He indicated he felt confident this would be the best course of action to treat the virus since a few of his transplant patients had developed the same virus and the treatment had worked for them. Dr. Del Toro then stated that the only problem with getting the treatment done was his hospital did not have the Hyperbaric Chamber. The hospital that had it was in the Bronx so we would have to travel there every morning for treatment. He added that before Najja started treatment, he would arrange for us to meet with the doctor in charge of the unit in order to discuss the procedure further.

One week later we were on our way to the Bronx to meet with the doctor in charge of the facility. Upon meeting her, she introduced herself as Dr. Wheng (name change). I immediately felt she was very cordial and inviting. As we sat down to talk, she reviewed Najja's history and then she began to explain the hyperbaric treatment procedure. She basically gave us the same information that Dr. Del Toro had given us. She added that most patients who had been exposed to that treatment usually had shown amazing post treatment results. She assured us that it was a fairly safe procedure, though; there were some risks from the treatment which included great pressure on the ears. She explained that in order to alleviate that pressure, Najja could drink some fluids then swallow really fast or she could pinch her nose then blow really hard several times. She also said that there were patients who had experienced seizures while doing the treatment but that only happened with patients who were prone to seizures or who were epileptics.

Dr. Wheng said that Najja should benefit from the treatments; therefore she should start treatment as soon as the insurance company had given the approval. I asked her how long it would take to get the approval from the insurance company. She said that it would take about four to five days. Dr. Wheng then took the time to give us a tour of the facility so that we could actually see what the Hyperbaric Chamber looked like. When we got to the actual room, the chamber was the first thing we saw. It was a deep blue, oblong shaped machine that looked exactly like a submarine. The inside resembled that of a small aircraft with cushioned seats and oxygen masks imbedded in the ceiling. I seized the opportunity to ask Dr. Wheng how long the Hyperbaric Therapy had been used to treat patients with chronic illness. She replied, "It has been used for several years, however the treatments are expensive and as a result, it is difficult to get the insurance companies to pay for them."

The meeting and the tour with Dr. Wheng was satisfying and informative for Najja and I since neither of us had any idea what a Hyperbaric Chamber or the treatment was. We thanked Dr. Wheng for her time and for giving us the information and the tour and then we left.

Within a week after the tour of the Bronx facility with the Hyperbaric Chamber, we received a call from Dr. Del Toro's secretary stating that the insurance company had given the approval for the hyperbaric treatment and that Najja could start her treatments immediately. The following morning we got ready and traveled to the Bronx. It was my mother, Najja, my husband and I who made the trip which took about an hour. When we got there the medical team was ready and waiting for Najja. The team consisted of a head nurse and two assistants. Before the treatment began, Najja's blood pressure and her pulse were taken. After her vital signs were taken it was time for her to go into the chamber. There were six other patients who were doing the treatment as well.

As she went into the chamber, she was separated from the other patients because of her compromised immune system. She was then given an oxygen mask to put over her nose and she had to remove her shoes for hygienic purposes. Once she and the other patients were ready for the treatment, one of the assistants accompanied them into the chamber to monitor their response to the treatment. While Najja did her treatment, my mother and I sat near the chamber quietly talking to each other and patiently waiting for her to finish. My husband on the other hand waited in his car however, he would come inside the room sporadically to find out how Najja was doing.

The treatment took about an hour and a half before it ended, then all the patients, including Najja exited the chamber. After the treatment, each patient had to be seen by the nurse or the assistants so that their vital signs could be checked before they were allowed to leave the site.

Day after day, we traveled to the Bronx, from January 13th to February 26th, so Najja could get the hyperbaric treatment. Then after she was finished with the hyperbaric treatment, we traveled to Manhattan to the clinic so that she could be seen by Dr. Del Toro. Once we got to the clinic, Najja's blood was drawn to make sure that her hemoglobin, white counts and platelets were at the appropriate levels. Her liver and kidneys were also monitored closely because of the medications she was taking. Her blood pressure and temperature were closely monitored, as well, for any signs of elevation.

Most days were long, we spent between seven and eight hours a day in treatment and travel time, it was frustrating, but we hung in there. We took it one step at a time and remained optimistic. Before we knew it Najja was done with the Hyperbaric Therapy and her bladder had healed. She was also taken off the Probenecid and Cidofovir. However, she continued to take her regular medications and her daily visits to the clinic were reduced to just twice a week because she was getting better day-by-day. Within three months, her clinic visits were reduced to just once a week and some of the medications were stopped.

By the end of May Najja had another setback. She started to complain from a pain in her right leg and she also had several small wart-like blisters on the inside of her right upper thigh. Of course we were not sure what they were so on the day of the clinic visit I showed them to Dr. Del Toro. He quickly recognized what they were. He said that she had developed a new virus. This one was known as Zoster Virus. It is part of the Chicken Pox family. He explained that many viruses are dormant in our bodies and when the immune system is compromised some of them surface and the Zoster Virus was one of them. He said that in order to treat it, Najja would have to be hospitalized for about seven days for antibiotic treatment via IV. Therefore, she was admitted the same day to start the treatment with an antibiotic called Acyclovir, which is an antiviral medication.

During her stay, she was monitored closely for any other complications. She made great progress and was discharged as planned on the seventh day. After her release, she continued to do well medically and otherwise. In fact, since she was making such great progress, Dr. Del Toro decided that she could go to her eight grade graduation ceremony that June. That was great news for Najja because she had not been to school since the transplant had started and she missed her friends and her school a lot. She had received home instructions to keep her abreast of her school work. I also asked Dr. Del Toro if she would be able to go to school in September. He hesitated to give her the approval to return to school because the original plan was for her to return in January 2011 as total recovery after a Bone Marrow Transplant took one full year for most patients. Anyway, by mid-August, Najja spoke to Dr. Del Toro again about returning to school. She stressed to him that she really wanted to go back to school because she had gone to her freshman orientation at her prospective high school and she was excited to start school.

Dr. Del Toro explained to her that the only way he would give her the release to return to school was if her immune system had returned to normal. He continued to explain to Najja that he would have to test her immune system (a special blood test) to see how strong it was and based on the results, she could actually go back to school by the end of September instead of January 2011. He added that once the test was done, it would take ten days for the results to come back. The results from the special blood test came back showing that her system was doing great and she was back to normal. So Dr. Del Toro gave Najja the release to return to school to September 29, 2010. She was so excited to go to high school for the first time and meet her new friends and new teachers.

It has been four years since Najja had the Bone Marrow Transplant and she has done and is still doing excellent. Health wise, she has had no other complications either from the transplant or the medications. She sees the hematologist once every six months just for an overall physical examine and routine blood work. It has been five years since the Bone Marrow Transplant and five and half years since the EDAS procedures. She sees Dr. G. the neurosurgeon once a year and each time he gives her a clean bill of health. Najja also sees a few other specialists just for routine annual visits.

In April of 2010, Najja's name was submitted to the Make-A-Wish Foundation® by the social worker from the hospital where she was being treated. Her name was submitted because she was considered to be one of those children who had a life threatening illness. Within a few weeks, representatives from the Foundation contacted Najja and asked to set up a meeting so they could talk to her about the greatest wish she would want. On the day of the meeting, two Make-A-Wish volunteers came to our home to meet with her. During the meeting, they talked with her about the history of the Foundation and some of the wonderful things it had done to make a difference in the lives of children who were very ill. They told Najja that they understood that she had gone through a lot and they thought she was a very brave girl. They also told her that she had the freedom to make at least two wishes and she should write them down in the order in which she wanted them and more than likely her first wish would be the one that would be granted. They went on and gave her examples of wishes other children were granted. They said that some children wished for shopping sprees, trips to Disney World, Caribbean vacations, and trips to the White

House to meet the President. Some kids wished to meet their favorite singers or movie stars. They mentioned quite a bit of wishes that were granted to children over the years. The volunteers explained to Najja that once she made her wishes, they would be presented to the Foundation for approval and once the approval was given they would contact her. Before the meeting ended, they told Najja to take some time to think out her wishes and once she had decided, she should contact them. It did not take Najja long before she decided on the wishes. Najja called her volunteers and told them that for her first wish, she wanted to go to Australia, and her second wish was a shopping spree. The volunteers advised Najja to fill out the wish paperwork and send it in to them. Once they received it, they would present her wishes to the Foundation. Within a few weeks, Najja received a call from her volunteers. They told her that her wish was approved for her to go to Australia and that she and all the members in her household would accompany her on the trip.

Not only was Najja excited, we were all excited for her. In April of 2011, Justin, my husband and I accompanied Najja to Sydney, Australia for 10 days. The trip was an awesome experience. We had the opportunity to tour the Sydney Harbour and the various landmarks in Sydney. We had several guided tours to the Blue Mountains and Sydney Wildlife Park, Bondi Beach, Koala Sanctuary and the Kangaroo Park, dolphin watching and a bus tour around Sydney. On the days that we were not on guided tours, we took the opportunity to tour the city ourselves. We visited places such as Sidney Business District, Chinatown, various museums, Darling Harbour, and the many restaurants.

Najja's trip to Australia was not only a memorable experience for her but it was a fantastic experience for the rest of the family as well. We needed time to restore our energy and reconnect as a family. We sincerely thank the Make-a-wish Foundation for granting Najja her wish.

About the Author

Kristin Walker holds a Bachelor's degree in Early Childhood Education and a Master's degree in Reading. She has worked in the public school system as a teacher for 20 years. Her passion for teaching led her to tutoring in an after-school setting, from home. This eventually led to opening a pre-school in Brooklyn, N.Y., which is still in operation today.

A wife and mother of four children, Kristin hopes that *My Daughter's Journey* will touch lives and bring healing.

Contact for Kristin at: mydaughtersjourney@yahoo.com or at (718) 986-0075.

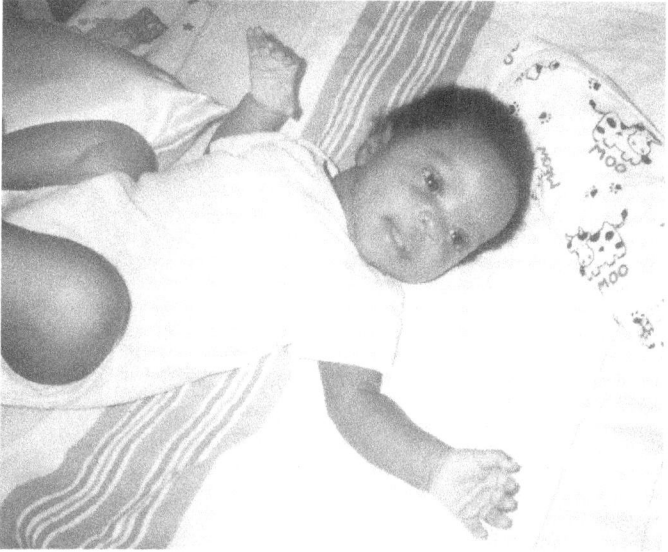

Najja's first month

Najja at 3 years old with Justin, 2 her potential donor

Najja at 6 years old with older sister Tishanna (left) and Aisha (right). Two days after being diagnose with stenosis of the carotid artery

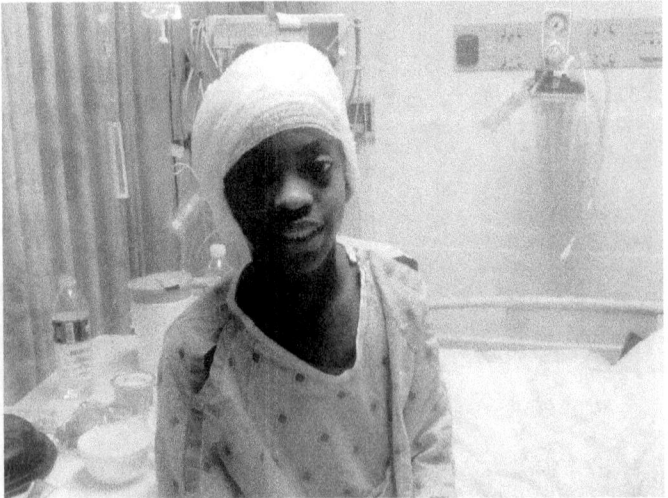

Najja at 11 years old. Three days after EDAS surgery

Najja and me one month before transplant

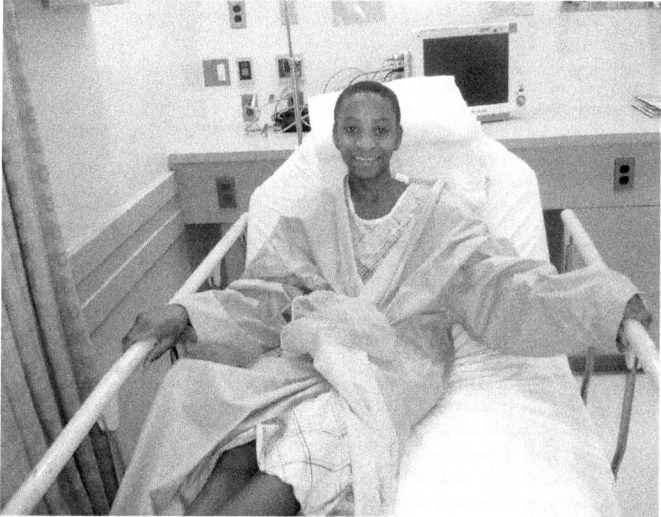

Justin, transplant day, preparing to give bone marrow

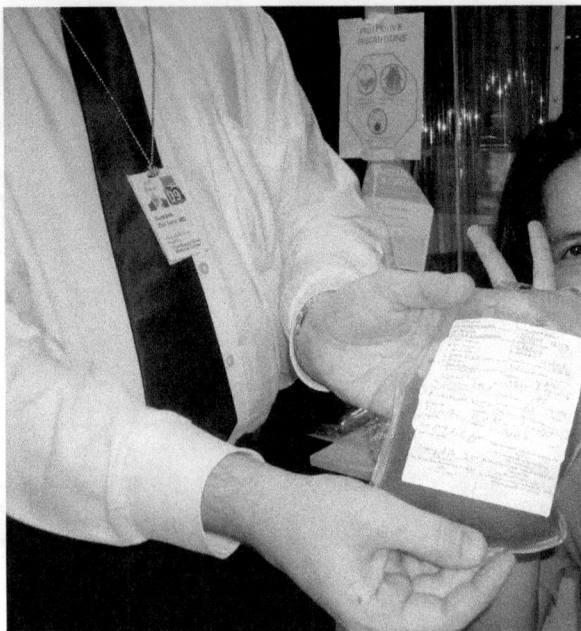

Treated bone marrow

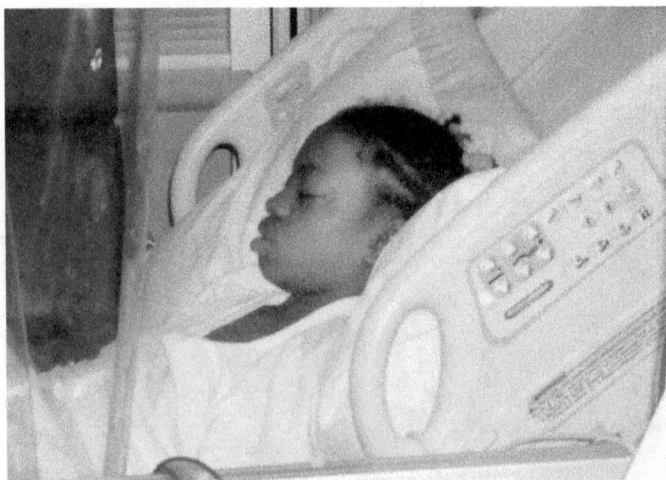

Najja one day after transplant

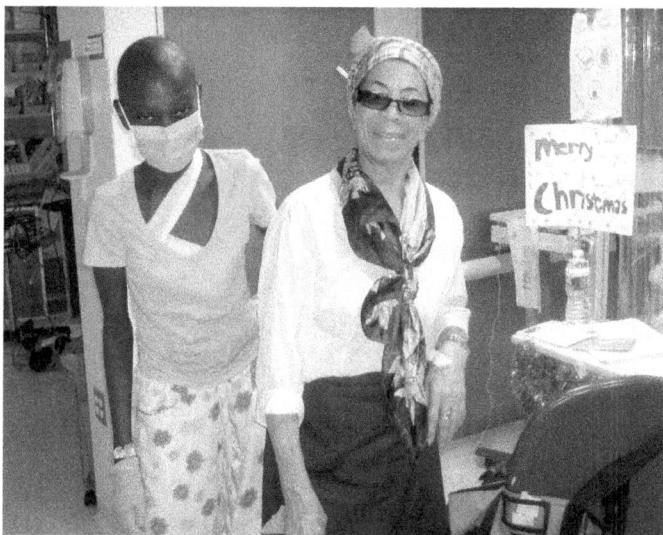

Najja and grandma Daphne (my mom), 3½ weeks after the transplant and the first day out of the special room

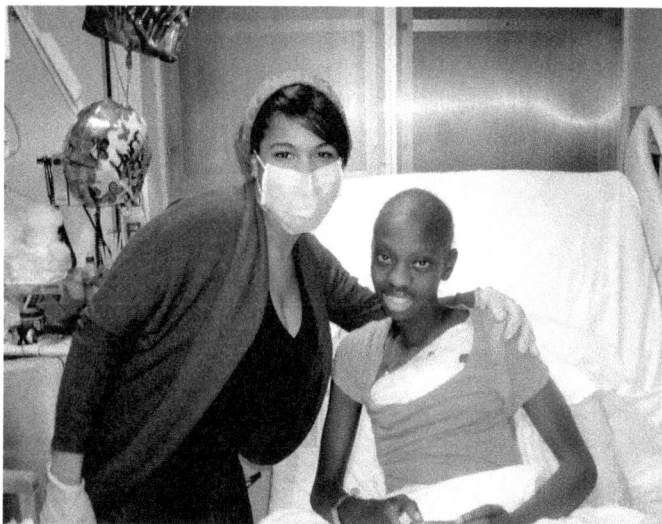

My niece, Shani and Najja

Trip to Australia - Najja at the Bondi Beach

Najja at the Kangaroo Santuary

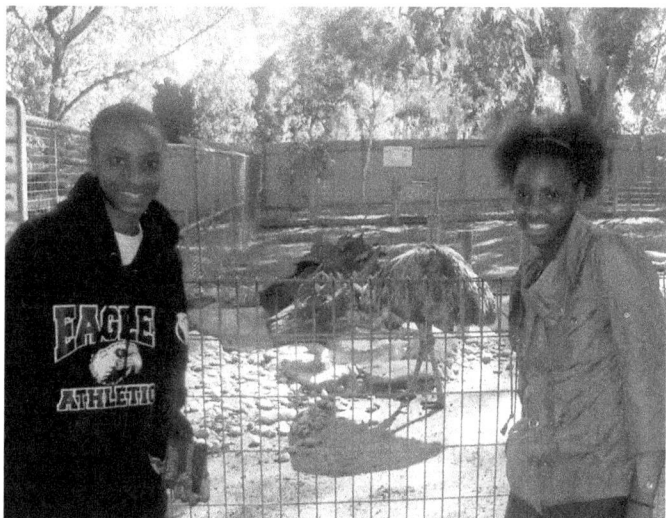

Najja and Justin at the Sydney Zoo

Our Family day trip at Sydney Harbor

Najja with her dad dancing at sweet 16

Najja and grandma Richards, (left,) and grandma Daphne (right)

Najja and her Godmother, Edmonde